A HEART TO DRUM

'Remarkable and ground-breaking initiative – listen, learn, and worship through it.'

Jeremy Begbie, Associate Principal, Ridley Hall, Cambridge; Professor of Theology, University of St Andrews

'*The Message* version of Psalm 66 encourages us to "set glory to the rhythms of His praise". Terl Bryant and the Psalm Drummers do just the same.'

Matt Redman, lead worshipper/songwriter

'In a global culture where rhythm is the soundtrack to millions of lives, I believe that the vision and ministry of Psalm Drummers is a powerful sign of God's heartbeat for redemption.'

Graham Kendrick, worship leader/songwriter

'Psalm Drummers combine the raw power of the ancient skill of percussion with a spiritual heart cry from deep within.'

Stewart Smith, drummer with Delirious?

'There is a new musical sound being birthed whose foundation is on ancient and traditional instruments. The heartbeat of this expression is the indigenous drum.'

Martin Neil, drummer, percussionist, producer

'Psalm Drummers bring a wonderfully exciting dimension to the joy, simplicity and compassion of knowing and praising God. The Psalms urge us to participate in the vast harmonious order that God has created, where all are called to sing the praises of the Almighty.'

John Sentamu, Archbishop of York

A Heart to Drum

For Psalm Drummers everywhere

TERL BRYANT

survivor

The majority of Bible quotations are taken from the New King
James Version of the Bible. Copyright Thomas Nelson, Inc.
Other quoted versions are indicated as follows: (NLT) New
Living Translation, (GNB) Good News Bible, (AB) Amplified
Bible, (NASB) New American Standard Bible.

ISBN 1 84291 335 2
13 ISBN 9781842913352

Survivor is an imprint of
KINGSWAY COMMUNICATIONS LTD
Lottbridge Drove, Eastbourne, BN23 6NT, England.
Email: books@kingsway.co.uk
Printed in Great Britain

Dedication

I give thanks first to my heavenly Father for the inspiration to drum – I believe it is a good gift (James 1:17).

I also want to dedicate this book with deep affection and in loving memory to my earthly father Terl M. Bryant (1929–2005). He was not a musician himself, but always encouraged me to drum, and I have many fond memories of the ways in which he did that. On one occasion when I was around eight years old, he inspired me in a way I will never forget. He was driving me to school in his sports car. He loved to play his music loud on the stereo and would thump out the beat on the steering wheel as he drove. As we pulled up near the school he heard a great drum fill in the track that was playing, and announced, 'Wow son, did you hear that? Fantastic!' He then rewound to listen to it again, and then again, and then again, and then again. As it played we both mimicked the fill in the air with our imaginary drumsticks. He was enthusiastic to the end, often coming to gigs and supporting me in all I did. I shall miss him.

Thanks

I would like to express a very special thanks to my dear Jules for hours of editing and offering invaluable additional comment that has helped shape this book.

Also to my friend Phil Manning, who corrected grammar and punctuation with his red pen, adding great encouragements throughout. Also to Jane Gregory for additional editing.

I want to thank all my dear drumming friends who added insightful comments in Chapter 8, and especially Chip Bailey, who stood with me throughout the first seven years of Psalm Drummers. Also Alun Leppitt, a great encourager and friend. Not forgetting a huge thank you to my many Psalm Drumming friends (too many to name) who have stood with me in this journey and especially those who make up the core network.

Contents

Foreword 11

Preface 13

1. The Bible Drum – Is There Such a Thing? 17
2. What the Bible Says About the Drum 29
3. Playing with Skill 40
4. Role Models and Influences 51
5. The Drummer's Psalm 70
6. Being a Psalm Drummer 102
7. The Voice of Drums 120
8. Personal Preparation and Application 139
9. Getting Out There 165
10. Practical Insights 180
11. Prayer 186

Suggested Reading and Resources 190
About the Author 191

Foreword

Drums make a lot of noise. They were designed that way. Throughout history drums have been used to make music and to convey messages. For me, they are a means of expressing an exuberant faith in response to the psalmist's invitation to 'make a joyful noise to God, all the earth'. Terl Bryant and I drum in harmony. We have done so in London and three times in Birmingham – including a BBC 1 service for Pentecost.

Terl founded Psalm Drummers, who accompanied me on my journey to Birmingham Cathedral when I was inaugurated as Bishop there in 2002, and again in 2005 on my voyage to York Minster as Archbishop, when on the coldest day imaginable we made our slow way by boat along the River Ouse. This rhythmic announcement of our arrival was greeted by excited crowds. In the service that followed, drummers from my home country of Uganda added their celebratory acclamations to the equally traditional music of church organ and other instruments.

It is my prayer that the message, the beat and above all the joy of drumming will be an offering to the God and Father of our Lord Jesus Christ, to whom be praise and glory for ever. May this book be a means to that end.

The Most Revd & Rt Hon Dr John Sentamu

Preface

Dear drummer or percussionist

If you are a follower of and believer in the Lord
Jesus Christ, regardless of denominational
background, race, age, musical taste or level of
playing experience; you need to know what God's
Word (the Bible) teaches about you and your gift.

Drums are played, offering a beat for all sorts of
music and activities, but what does God really say
about drumming? People often describe the drum as
the oldest instrument in the world. Is that really
true? Is it just an interesting fact that every day,
almost everywhere in the world, people hear
drumming? Why, out of the many thousands of
people who enjoy drumming, are so few fulfilled?
And where are the drums in the Bible?

Scripture repeatedly encourages us to make music and to delight in the Lord – and there are numerous scriptures about singing and expressing our praise and worship in song. But what of the drum? Are we to assume the Psalms were only ever accompanied by melodic instruments? Has drumming become acceptable in our times only as part of the contemporary church's approach to music?

The biggest book in the Bible is the book of Psalms. It is a book of songs, largely attributed to a man who started out in life from humble roots. He was the youngest son of a Bethlehem farmer who, through obedience to God, rose to be the greatest king of all time. King David is described in Scripture as follows:

> **He raised up for them David as king, to whom also He gave testimony and said, 'I have found David the son of Jesse, a man after My own heart, who will do all My will.'**
>
> **(Acts 13:22)**

Described as 'a man after God's heart', King David followed God's instruction and established the most renowned worshipping community recorded in history. He then chose a percussionist to oversee it. (See Chapter 4 on Asaph.)

As you read on, I pray you will be encouraged and envisioned through God's Word and His heart for you in your drumming. The Lord knows who you are, and yes, He does have a plan for you:

> **For I know the thoughts that I think toward you, says the LORD, thoughts of peace and not of evil, to give you a future and a hope.**
>
> **(Jeremiah 29:11)**

All God's promises are true (Psalm 33:4–5). He is the way, the truth and the life (John 14:6). If we do it His way according to His Word we will succeed (Deuteronomy 28:1–2).

I hope this book will serve as a valuable tool to inspire you in your drumming.

Peace and grace,
Terl Bryant

CHAPTER 1

The Bible Drum – Is There Such a Thing?

Have you ever been asked, 'So, where are the drums in the Bible?'

During the early 1980s, and soon after I had come to Christ, I started playing drums in the Christian music scene. I was living in Orange County, California, and joined the Steve Taylor Band as Steve's touring drummer. Steve and his band (known as Some Band) were making waves in US gospel music, characterised by the then edgy New Wave sound that was hitting America with artists like Elvis Costello, The Cars, Talking Heads, etc. Yes, you're right. It was a long time ago. I was still in my early twenties and in 1984 Steve had a Billboard number one hit with a song called 'Hero'. We were busy touring the States doing concerts on his Colour Code tour at Christian festivals and events countrywide. The experience was amazing; it far exceeded all my expectations of what it must be like working in a popular rock band. I was fulfilling my dreams and working with wonderful guys who were dedicated to the Lord. The travel was also eye-opening. I was to meet every conceivable kind of 'so-called' believer you could imagine. Many left me inspired with incredible stories and genuine humility, but as a new believer I was deeply disappointed to discover how many would talk the talk but clearly not walk the walk. It was a big learning curve.

We arrived at a large church venue somewhere in one of the southern states in the middle of the tour. I was setting up drums early in the afternoon while the rest of the band was still out eating. I was in the huge auditorium by myself, taking my time and enjoying working at a relaxed pace (so much of the tour had been go, go, go!). As I was quite happily working away I noticed someone enter through the furthest doors at the back. They started walking down the central aisle towards me. It was a lady, an older lady, and she was carrying a glass of water. She was definitely coming my way, so I thought, 'How nice. She's bringing me a drink.' But then as she drew near I could see she was clearly focused and looked a bit scary! It all happened so quickly. I suddenly braced myself and then before I knew it . . . I was soaked! The lady threw the water over me and with intense authority and a shrill tone she commanded, 'Demon, come out! Come out, you evil spirit of drumming, right now in the name of Jesus!'

Well, you can imagine, I was a little shocked. I remained quite still as I watched her turn and march all the way back down the aisle and out of the room. I don't recall saying a word; I just thought, 'Whoa . . . there are some extraordinary people out there!'

But it did start me thinking more seriously about my role as a drummer. It made me think, for perhaps the first time, that I needed to find out more. In a roundabout way I am grateful to the lady (God loves her and so must I) because it was this that really prompted me to go and do a bit of study. I really had to ask myself, 'Could I have got it all wrong, or is there actually some biblical support beyond the feel-good factor in bashing these drums?' So here we go. . .

Where are the drums in the Bible?

There are in fact seventeen references in Scripture to the Hebrew word *tof*, which modern translators mostly interpret as 'tambourine', or sometimes 'timbrel' or 'tabret'.

The *tof* (a word still used today by orthodox Jews) is very like our contemporary word 'drum', in that it does not define the instrument in every detail. It is the name given for the common drum of the period, a frame drum. Although often decorated, it is an historic and simple design, being a skin fixed over a circular frame that is larger in diameter than depth. Frame drums are common all over the world and in biblical times would have varied in size and depth, as they do today. The name '*tof*', like most drums throughout the world, is onomatopoeic. That simply means it describes the sound it makes. Think of other drum names like 'conga', 'tumba', 'doumbek', 'tar', 'tom-tom' and even the word 'drum'. A linguist or Hebrew scholar is likely to comment that the *tof* would not have had jingles, as there is no metallic quality in the sound of its name. Contrast that to the metallic resonance of the word 'tambourine'. 'Tambour' is the drum sound, and 'rine' suggests the metallic sound. It may also be worth mentioning that *tambour* remains the French word for drum.

This now opens the box of percussion to enable us to look a little deeper.

There are commonly two types of frame drums across the globe: plain drums, whose primary sound comes from the skin, like the Middle Eastern 'tar', Egyptian 'duff', and South Indian 'kanjira'; and those with additional sound-makers attached, commonly metal ring chains, bells or jingles, which are attached to the rim, or inset into the frame. The Egyptian 'riq' (or 'rek'), Brazilian 'pandiero', and the 'tamburello' found in Spain and Italy, are common drums that feature the metallic sounds of jingles. Other drums like the North African 'bendir' can have a gut string (an early form of snare) underneath and the 'tambores con charchillos' are Peruvian drums with vibrating cactus spines underneath.

Percussion Instruments and Their History by the late James Blades (originally published in 1969 by Faber & Faber) also refers to instruments of Mesopotamia and Egypt circa 1100 BC. These include frame drums, small kettledrums (baz) and vase-shaped drums made of clay. Blades supports the view that the biblical tof had no jingles. He comments, 'In Biblical references the words tinkling and metal are used in connection with bells and cymbals, but not with tabret or timbrel (commonly translated as tambourine).'

So why do translations of the Bible speak of a tambourine and not simply a drum?

The name 'tambourine' does have historic roots, being a generic name for differing sizes of frame drum with jingles common throughout Europe for several hundred years. However, the tambourine has been popularised in Western culture as the name for a lightweight jingle instrument often lacking a head or skin. With a skin it is limited to finger drumming due to its delicate nature.

This is where the problems of definition really start to arise. It seems the tambourine has been

going through some changes (haven't we all?) and
that the drummer and the tambourine player of
today have much less in common than several
hundred years ago. The point is, when we read
about the tambourine in the Bible it is all too easy to
imagine a rather nice, rather safe, rather ineffective
and inconsequential little jingly noise going along
with the music, instead of the authority and focus
of a dedicated and professional drummer, playing a
powerful beat on a large frame drum to empower
the music – a beat that reflects the passion of the
Psalms and the almighty nature of God!

However, the strongest argument for the
character of the *tof* still remains its name, which
most naturally indicates a deep thud. Try saying it.
It's not 'tar', 'tif', 'tick', 'tom', 'ching', 'ping' or
anything else – '*tof*' is a very definite drum sound.
The popular Irish frame drum, the bodhran
(pronounced 'bow-ron'), is very close in sound.
Incidentally, whenever I've been to Ireland
everyone seems to say the name differently – and
use a different implement to play it: anything from a
little carefully turned stick to a favourite old
paintbrush! Making this connection between the *tof*

and bodhran is really quite interesting, as some historians believe the instrument made its way to Ireland from the Middle East in ancient times. It is also probable that the Bible *tof* would have been played with hands and/or with sticks according to the natural preference of the player, not unlike many ethnic drums today. Indeed, most drummers of today have a stick bag containing a wide variety of sticks, mallets, brushes and other playing implements.

We mustn't forget either that 'tambourine' is only one of the words used in English Bible translations. The authoritative King James and the New King James Bibles use 'tabret' or 'timbrel'. These words seem to create less of an issue when translated as 'drum', closing the gap for misunderstandings, even though they are not commonly used today.

In light of this it becomes clear that the use of the English word 'tambourine' is at best incomplete and at worst misleading. It is clearly outdated and fails to describe accurately the instrument found in the Bible. In respect of the modern drummer, it is not simply a minor technical oversight: it stands as a fundamental travesty, which arguably hinders the

authority of the ancient texts reaching an immense
number of gifted drummers throughout the world
in our times. There are many thousands of faithful
and gifted men and women who hold a calling to
strike the drum according to God's Word. The
translation for *tof* rendered 'tambourine' essentially
misrepresents the drum that appears in God's Word
an impressive seventeen times.

In Old Testament times the *tof* was often played
by women and associated with dance. Norman
A. Rubin, a Christian writer living in Israel writing
for bibarch.com (a website on biblical archaeology),
raises a point of interest worth mentioning. He
notes that after the destruction of the Temple
(586 BC), Jewish tradition opposed the use of the *tof*-
drum out of the fearful belief that being connected
to women and dance, it was therefore associated
with temptation and corruption! Here enters the
religious spirit, which is always out to steal the joy
of the Lord. Although this view is clearly
repressive, it may serve to remind us to act
responsibly with the gifts we are entrusted with.

Another common misconception is that the drum
set (or drum kit) is either separate from, or indeed

superior to, the wider family and variety of hand drums and percussion instruments found throughout the world. This is probably due to the dominant presence of drum sets in Western popular music. Admittedly the drum set, presented in a highly polished, sparkly fancy finish with all sorts of extra bits and bobs attached, will impress. The level of multi-tasking required to play it is also not in question. However, there is a real danger of pride visiting the modern drummer, who can think he or she is in some way superior to drummers of old.

Although due respect is in order for those players who have studied and developed extraordinary levels of skill in playing the drum set (some can offer a display that will compete with the opening of the Olympics!), the idea that it is superior remains short-sighted and can easily be countered in light of its history. The drum set, largely developed in the USA and to a lesser degree in Western Europe, is surprisingly no more than 100 years old. This relative baby has developed fundamentally through rock and jazz music since World War One. It is conversely not a new invention, being merely a grouping of ancient instruments that are now manufactured by one of a number of specialist companies – hence the uniformity of image. This is also how it has developed its more common description of being (singular) a drum 'set' (or drum 'kit') rather than the more accurate title 'a set of drums'. Although the technology and construction has changed and keeps changing, the basic sounds of each instrument remain very similar to the instruments of old.

With all this in mind, the bottom line is that the church has, on the whole, been ignorant of the importance and power in worship and warfare of drums. Just think of all the gifted drummers throughout history who have been refused a part in the declaration of praise that is due to our great and mighty Lord. Think of the many platforms that have preached drumming as 'of the devil'. Although God waits patiently to impart wisdom, we are wise to seek it. With wisdom and revelation we can hear the Lord's heart on these things and know what is good in His sight.

I beseech you therefore, brethren, by the mercies of God, that you present your bodies a

living sacrifice, holy, acceptable to God, which is your reasonable service. And do not be conformed to this world, but be transformed by the renewing of your mind, that you may prove what is that good and acceptable and perfect will of God.

(Romans 12:1–2)

CHAPTER 2

What the Bible Says About the Drum

'For the word of the Lord is right, and all His work is done in truth.'

(Psalm 33:4–6)

The drum is widely thought of and sometimes referred to as the oldest instrument in the world. Why is that exactly? It could possibly be true, but as far as I know there is no proof one way or another. The first instruments referred to in Scripture are in fact the harp and flute in Genesis 4:21. I do, however, believe that there is a significant deception at work in labelling the drum as the oldest instrument.

The suggestion seems to conjure up the image of a hunched, hairy, short, ox-like man. His eyes are deeply set and his expression is, shall we say, 'vacant'. He is wearing a furry short dress made of cowhide (ouch), and he is holding two over-sized clubs that thicken towards the ends. His matted hair is everywhere and keeps getting tangled in the dog bone that he has pierced his nose with. He is hopping like a mad fool from leg to leg, beating a large hollow log – and is wearing a bizarre grin. In another million years (his paradiddles should be quite good by then), he will have cut the end of the hollow log off and stretched a spare piece of skin (perhaps the fleshy tablecloth from his cave) over the tree trunk to make the first membraphone (the technical term for a drum). The modern world is affectionately cheering him on, thinking he will one day catch up with the rest of society.

You see – is that really the truth?

I believe Genesis 1:26, which says, 'Then God said, "Let Us make man in Our image, according to Our likeness; let them have dominion. . .",' and verse 28: 'Then God blessed them, and God said to them, "Be fruitful and multiply; fill the earth and subdue it."'

Is our so-called 'early man' made in the image of God? Is he like God? When looking around at the beauty and detail of the Lord's handiwork in Genesis, did the Lord pop this, our first drummer, into the midst of all that He had made? I am afraid it is here also that the plethora of drummers' jokes are born – I'm sure you've heard a few.

Out of the ground the LORD God formed every beast of the field and every bird of the air, and brought them to Adam to see what he would call them. And whatever Adam called each living creature, that was its name.

(Genesis 2:19)

Do you get my point? God created man *in His image,* to be intelligent and communicative. God spoke with him and walked with him, and man quickly developed in close-knit, organised communities. 'Then God blessed them, and God said to them, "Be fruitful and multiply; fill the earth and subdue it."' These people, drummers among them, were not some lower form of life. They were like us.

Genesis 4:19–22 talks about Adam's immediate descendants having skills for making musical instruments, working with metals and raising herds. The first reference for drumming is in Genesis 31:27, which shows drums and stringed instruments being played together as an integral part of their culture: 'Why did you flee away secretly, and steal away from me, and not tell me; for I might have sent you away with joy and songs, with timbrel and harp?' (Genesis 31:27).

The Bible does not tell us the drum is the oldest instrument. The exciting truth is that God's Word does tell us a good deal about drumming – and gives authority for the drummer to strike the drum in celebration, praise, worship and more. Through reading and studying each of the seventeen references to the *tof* found later in this chapter, we can gain understanding, grow in wisdom and find God's will; His good and perfect will for the drummer.

All Scripture is given by inspiration of God, and is profitable for doctrine, for reproof, for correction, for instruction in righteousness, that the man of God may be complete, thoroughly equipped for every good work.

(2 Timothy 3:16)

Before going through this list, however, here in brief are some quick references for the drum being played in various contexts:

- 1 Chronicles 13:8 – in praise
- Psalm 150:4 – in worship
- Psalm 68:25 – for prophecy
- 1 Samuel 10:5–6 – in remembrance and freedom
- Psalm 81:2–7 – in declaration of the Lord's sovereignty
- Isaiah 30:32 – for spiritual warfare

The seventeen references for '*tof*' on page 36 are found in the common English translations. The last reference is only found in the King James and New King James English translations, where it forms part of the description of the pre-fallen archangel Lucifer, who is Satan!

The list of references should serve to encourage us and also to warn us. Drumming is clearly a powerful activity, it is a forthright expression and it is bold and imposing. When the drummer plays, those present are always affected. The beat demands a response and you either have to go with it, or get away from it! The power of rhythm is in God's design. Rhythm is at work throughout all God has made. It is visibly at work in the order of the universe right through to the tiniest of insects. This in itself is a huge and wonderful study for another day. However, I would like us to see today at least something of the power of it – and, in turn, the power of drumming.

Think for a moment how the rhythmic movement of the planets creates the seasons, how the rhythm of the tide creates sand from the rocks on the seashore, how an army marching in unison displays authority and power, how a heart beating with adrenalin enables the runner in the race, how a drummer playing with zeal will stir the atmosphere in a concert hall. The power of rhythm is at work in each of these examples. It causes change, and affects what it comes into contact with. It is a principle of God's making.

It is something for the drummer to recognise and take hold of. The player holds the responsibility for exercising their rhythmic 'voice' through the character of the beat, the sound and the effect it creates. Good or bad, it remains powerful.

May your beat serve Jehovah, our great and mighty God, in joy, in praise and in obedience. If it does not serve Him, it will serve the enemies of God. It is your choice. 'The LORD has given you a heart to perceive and eyes to see and ears to hear, to this very day' (Deuteronomy 29:4).

Through lack of knowledge, drummers have provided the beat for the song of the enemy. They and their drumming have also been misunderstood, controlled, stifled and misused in the world and within the church. It is through God's Word that we gain access to the truth, learning to discern between good and evil, finding and understanding our purpose and the authority truly to be who we are made to be: 'If you abide in My word, you are My disciples indeed. And you shall know the truth, and the truth shall make you free' (John 8:31–32).

Reading the following references alone is not enough. Please study the surrounding chapters and access the context for them. Ask the Lord for revelation and understanding in relation to your role as a drummer or percussionist. Each of these drumming moments is there to learn from and will add insight to your gift. As you take them in, you will have greater authority and freedom to play.

1. *Genesis 31:27* 'Why did you flee away secretly, and steal away from me, and not tell me; for I might have sent you away with joy and songs, with timbrel [*tof*] and harp?'

2. *Exodus 15:20* 'Then Miriam the prophetess, the sister of Aaron, took the timbrel [*tof*] in her hand; and all the women went out after her with timbrels [*tof*] and with dances.'

3. *Judges 11:34* 'When Jephthah came to his house at Mizpah, there was his daughter, coming out to meet him with timbrels [*tof*] and dancing; and she was his only child. Besides her he had neither son nor daughter.'

4. *1 Samuel 10:5* 'After that you shall come to the hill of God where the Philistine garrison is. And it will happen, when you have come there to the city, that you will meet a group of prophets coming down from the high place with a stringed instrument, a tambourine [*tof*], a flute, and a harp before them; and they will be prophesying.'

5. *1 Samuel 18:6* 'Now it had happened as they were coming home, when David was returning from the slaughter of the Philistine, that the women had come out of all the cities of Israel, singing and dancing, to meet King Saul, with tambourines [*tof*], with joy, and with musical instruments.'

6. *2 Samuel 6:5* 'Then David and all the house of Israel played music before the LORD on all kinds of instruments of fir wood, on harps, on stringed instruments, on tambourines [*tof*], on sistrums, and on cymbals.'

7. *1 Chronicles 13:8* 'Then David and all Israel played music before God with all their might, with singing, on harps, on stringed instruments, on tambourines [*tof*], on cymbals, and with trumpets.'

8. *Job 21:12* 'They sing to the tambourine [*tof*] and harp, And rejoice to the sound of the flute.'

9. *Psalm 68:25* 'The singers went before, the players on instruments followed after; among them were the maidens playing timbrels [*tof*].'

10. *Psalm 81:2* 'Raise a song and strike the timbrel [*tof*], the pleasant harp with the lute.'

11. *Psalm 149:3* 'Let them praise His name with the dance; let them sing praises to Him with the timbrel [*tof*] and harp.'

12. *Psalm 150:4* 'Praise Him with the timbrel [*tof*] and dance; praise Him with stringed instruments and flutes.'

13. *Isaiah 5:12* 'The harp and the strings, the tambourine [*tof*] and flute, and wine are in their feasts; but they do not regard the work of the LORD, nor consider the operation of His hands.'

14. *Isaiah 24:8* 'The mirth of the tambourine [*tof*] ceases, the noise of the jubilant ends, the joy of the harp ceases.'

15. *Isaiah 30:32* 'And in every place where the staff of punishment passes, which the LORD lays on him, it will be with tambourines [*tof*] and harps; and in battles of brandishing He will fight with it.'

16. *Jeremiah 31:4* 'Again I will build you, and you shall be rebuilt, O virgin of Israel! You shall again be adorned with your tambourines [*tof*], and shall go forth in the dances of those who rejoice.'

17. *Ezekiel 28:13* 'You were in Eden, the garden of God; every precious stone was your covering:

the sardius, topaz, and diamond, beryl, onyx, and jasper, sapphire, turquoise, and emerald with gold. The workmanship of your timbrels [*tof*] and pipes was prepared for you on the day you were created.'

Now put God's Word into action. As an exercise, memorise three drum scriptures. Look up the wider context and personalise them – speak them out to yourself before you play. Decide to align yourself with God's Word and His will for you as a drummer or percussionist. Here are three examples that might be helpful, but also choose your own. Ask the Lord to inspire you.

1. 'I will praise His name with the dance; I will sing praises to Him with my drums' (Psalm 149:3, personalised).
2. 'I will join the prophets coming down from the high place with my drum and will prophesy that God is with us' (1 Samuel 10:5, 7, personalised).
3. 'With my drum I will join the procession of my God into His sanctuary' (Psalm 68:24–25, personalised).

CHAPTER 3

Playing with Skill

'Chenaniah, leader of the Levites, was instructor in charge of the music, because he was skilful.'

(1 Chronicles 15:22)

'Praise the LORD with the harp; make melody to Him with an instrument of ten strings. Sing to Him a new song; play skilfully with a shout of joy.'

(Psalm 33:2–3).

If you have a musical gift, the Bible calls you to invest in it. Naturally it is your choice. No one will force you to do it (at least I hope not), but if it is God's gift, then surely we should honour Him by polishing it. While keen novices should always be encouraged, think how much more you could enhance the music by developing your skill.

You are in church, ready to sing with passion a song of worship to the most high God. The bandleader starts with some opening chords on the acoustic guitar, and then, without warning, there is a coal delivery on the drums! It sounds as if someone has thrown a cupboard full of pots and pans down a flight of stairs, ending with the most painful damage at the bottom. As the song continues, your eyes are squeezed tightly shut in a vain attempt to shut out the distraction and focus on the glorious lyrics of praise. . .and then at the end of the first verse, leading into the chorus, it happens again. . .only worse! The over-excited and rather wide-eyed drummer has just crashed entirely past the downbeat of the chorus, hitting somewhere between beats two and three a bar late! The whole congregation braces – faithfully determined to press on. The worship leader remains utterly focused, although his fingers are now raw as he grates them on the wire strings to hold the beat together. The keyboard player loses it as her eyes pass from exasperating looks at her family seated on the front row to glaring vindictive looks at the drummer. . . who is now totally crushed. His only response is to play even louder in a last attempt to put it all right. . .oh no!

Been there?

There is another side. You are in church, ready to sing with passion a song of worship to the most high God. The bandleader starts with some opening chords on the acoustic guitar, and then . . . the performance starts. You open your mouth, making the shape of the first word in the lyric, and to your horror several extra bars of intensely clever, over-rehearsed pushes and stabs have been added in. You open your eyes, naturally looking for some helpful cue, because the odd-time meter (known only to the advanced musicians on the stage) has thrown you completely off balance. Then you notice (because you hadn't really before) that the worship leader's shirt is open to the middle of his chest and his head is turned, offering a pouting smirk of approval to the drummer, who has delivered an intense fill (a run of sixty-fourth notes) around a range of tom-toms (4′, 6′, 8′, 10′, 12′, 14′, 16′, 18′, plus some others he's knocked up in his workshop) at the end of the extraordinarily over-the-top, musically brilliant, but completely self-focused worship song.

Yikes ... that hurt!

We need wisdom to get it right. What, indeed, does 'getting it right' involve? First, let's forget trying to create a rulebook.

For the law of the Spirit of life in Christ Jesus has made me free from the law of sin and death.

(Romans 8:2)

For you, brethren, have been called to liberty; only do not use liberty as an opportunity for the flesh, but through love serve one another.

(Galatians 5:13)

I want to talk about the scriptural call to play with skill and what that really means. Many have failed to find a healthy balance in this area. It has become a trap for some, who get overly focused on perfecting their skill, and then, in turn, dismiss the honest expression of others who apparently don't measure up. Others may not even get started, feeling they will never be good enough in the eyes of the so-called skilful.

Again it is in God's Word that we will find the answers we need, but we must be prepared for a little study: as we delve deeper into the original context and meaning of words we will grow in understanding. We need to know the Lord's heart so that we can bring an appropriate offering to Him in our drumming, music-making, and praise and worship.

In the opening verse of this chapter (1 Chronicles 15:22) Chenaniah, leader of the Levites, held a position of leadership as an instructor '. . .because he was skilful'. This could easily be misinterpreted based on our understanding of the word 'skill'. The word here in the Hebrew is *sakal* (pronounced 'saw-kal'), and gives us more insight into why Chenaniah was given the office of instructor. It is also why we in turn must learn to play with *sakal* and not just skill.

The word *sakal* means 'wisely understand, prosper, to have insight, to give attention to, consider, having comprehension, to be prudent or circumspect'.

Sakal appears in Scripture a total of sixty-three times, most commonly translated into English as 'wise', 'prosper' and 'understand', but only twice as 'skill'. Here are three examples, with the word translated from *sakal* in italics:

> So when the woman saw that the tree was good for food, that it was pleasant to the eyes, and a tree desirable to make one *wise*, she took of its fruit and ate.
>
> (Genesis 3:6, italics mine)

> Therefore keep the words of this covenant, and do them, that you may *prosper* in all that you do.
>
> (Deuteronomy 29:9, italics mine)

> For God is the King of all the earth; sing praises with *understanding*.
>
> (Psalm 47:7, italics mine)

Psalm 33 also refers to playing skilfully. In verse 3 the writer states, 'Play skilfully with a shout of joy.' The word here is another Hebrew word, *yatab,* that has similarities to *sakal. Yatab* means 'to do well, do thoroughly, to make a thing good or right or beautiful'.

Although very valuable, skill in itself is not enough; we need to develop a *sakal* mindset for our playing. The following two lists help us to see how this works. They are not necessarily in order of importance, but they are typical of the kind of response I have had from my students when studying this question.

To play drums with *sakal* is to play with:

- a heart open to the Holy Spirit;
- wisdom;
- understanding;
- obedience;
- consideration;
- sensitivity;
- passion;
- appropriateness;
- care and empathy;
- authority;
- patience;
- skill;
- technique.

To play drums with skill is to play with:

- technique;
- musical knowledge;
- advanced study;
- speed and dexterity;

- control;
- experience;
- good musicianship;
- professional attitude.

Can you see how playing with *sakal* is to play with *spiritual wisdom and humility,* and playing with skill is something that can be done excellently *without any sensitivity or connection to the heart*? I am in no way suggesting that we ignore the value of playing skilfully, but it must always be subject to *sakal*. You can see that the characteristics of the word 'skill' are mostly functional, and the characteristics of *sakal* are much more about the heart.

> **Who may ascend into the hill of the LORD? Or who may stand in His holy place? He who has clean hands and a pure heart, who has not lifted up his soul to an idol.**
>
> **(Psalm 24:3– 4)**

I had a moment of revelation one night as my wife Jules and I sat down for supper together. It had been a long day, we were both tired and we had just got the children tucked up in bed. Almost as soon as we sat down, the door to the living room creaked open and a little face peeped round. It was our son Louis, then about four years of age. I was just about to exercise my parental authority and send him back up the stairs, when I stopped. He looked very sweet, so I invited him to come and sit on my knee while we ate. He was as good as gold (of course) and soon we had finished eating. I said, 'Louis, be a good boy now and get yourself back to bed.' He obediently jumped off my knee and crossed the room to do as I had asked. Just before he left, he turned and said, 'Daddy . . .' I smiled back and then he said, 'I really, really love you.' It was a very special moment – all daddies love to hear their children tell them how much they love them.

When I thought this through, I realised how relevant it is in terms of worship and in terms of *sakal*.

First, Louis was only four. He didn't have a sophisticated vocabulary, he hadn't achieved huge worldly success, he wasn't well travelled or very experienced. He was just a little boy. Clearly he wasn't ready to take the stage for the Sunday morning sermon, but no one could criticise what he had told his daddy. There can be no greater offering than a child telling his or her father, 'I love you.' It is the essence of worship and the essence of *sakal*. The timing, relevance, appropriateness, honesty, self-sacrifice and beauty of it was beyond judgement. It was a perfect moment.

Can you tell your heavenly Father, with your drums, 'Daddy, I really, really love You'?

But the hour is coming, and now is, when the true worshippers will worship the Father in spirit and truth; for the Father is seeking such to worship Him.

(John 4:23)

The Bible is calling us to search out truth and gain a deeper understanding of our drumming so we may reflect, and rise to, a vision of God's holiness. This is not about becoming some sort of stiff-necked overly serious musician who resides in the lofty places of super-spirituality. The Lord is not asking you to throw away the freedom and joy you find in drumming. The complete opposite is true. The Lord is calling us into deeper joy, deeper freedom and the place of radical power where He allows us to join

the glorious sound of His heavenly choir in praise.
Let us be abandoned to complete obedience and
discover together the groove of eternity: God's
heartbeat!

Role Models and Influences

In Scripture we have two important 'drummer' role models in Asaph and Miriam. Who were Asaph and Miriam, and what is their relevance for us today? Before getting to know them a bit, let's first look at the power of role models.

We would all agree that those around us influence us, whether we like it or not. The first and strongest influences naturally come from our parents or those who have looked after us in what are called 'the formative years'. There is a saying, 'Show me the boy and I will show you the man', which suggests that the qualities we have in adulthood are formed very early on. Many doctors and educationalists, including Dr Maria Montessori and the US

Department for Health and Human Services, present the period from birth to age seven as our greatest period of growth, mentally and physically. These are the years that contribute most to the shaping of our character and personality.

Thank God this is not definitive though. The Lord Jesus is a restorer and healer. Many Christians have a story to testify to the transformation in their lives that following Christ and feeding on His Word produces. Christians need to know that we don't have to be the product of our background:

> **Therefore, if anyone is in Christ, he is a new creation; old things have passed away; behold, all things have become new.**
>
> **(2 Corinthians 5:17)**

This transforming work is not just referring to our salvation and the promise of eternal life – though that is of course immense good news; it is also referring to our literal transformation, a process that can start today! Those things that have held us back and kept us bound can be broken and beaten so that we can enjoy the freedom of being who God originally made us to be. However, this will not happen unless it is taken hold of in faith and action.

Imagine that a good friend told you that his house was open for you to come and enjoy and use; that it was full of food, clothes and everything you could ever want; but then you always drove by, never feeling quite good enough to visit, always thinking he would prefer someone else to use it. In that case you wouldn't really know or trust your friend, and the only one to miss out would be you! Deep down you wanted better, but taking that step of faith seemed a bit scary: 'I don't feel worthy to go in there. It's much too grand. What if I do something wrong, or touch something I'm not supposed to?' The Lord's restoring work is like that. He offers you 'good gifts' freely. He offers to bless you, restore you, overwhelm you with His goodness; but you need to take a little courage and actively work with Him.

Oh, taste and see that the Lord is good.

(Psalm 34:8)

Then Jesus spoke to them again, saying, 'I am the light of the world. He who follows Me

shall not walk in darkness, but have the light of life.'

(John 8:12)

Going back to looking at our childhood years, part of the process must be to understand, to some extent, what went on in those years and the influential power of role models, both good and bad.

Jesus cares passionately that each child of His should thrive. He knows each one intimately and holds great hopes and dreams for them, just like any good parent. He knows the special qualities and gifts He has placed in each unique one, and He knows the real implications of a child's wellbeing. He warned:

Whoever causes one of these little ones who believe in Me to sin, it would be better for him if a millstone were hung around his neck, and he were drowned in the depth of the sea.

(Matthew 18:6)

That's strong stuff, isn't it? For many the hardest struggle is accepting God's love, yet everywhere you look in God's Word you can see His passionate love. It isn't just for those people who are really good, those who look nice, those born in the right place and the right time. He loves you just because you are you. Remember, He made you and He doesn't make rubbish.

Yes, there is room for improvement – so let Him improve you! That's called obedience. But stop feeling sorry for yourself. You are not lower than anyone else. That is a lie! The most high God loves YOU.

'But, but, but. . .' NO BUTS. He loves YOU.

He forgives all your sins, heals all your diseases, redeems your life from destruction. He crowns you with His loving kindness and tender mercies.

(Psalm 103:3–4, paraphrased)

A principle for the healthy development of every child, alongside love, affirmation, touch, communication, etc., is encouragement to learn. This is the founding principle behind our entire education system: that through learning we might reach our potential in life. Not surprisingly this can, and often does, become a stumbling block in its own right, but it is folly to ignore the importance of education. It is clearly God's plan that we should be outward looking, always wanting to learn and interested in the function and form of all that He has made.

> **The Lord by wisdom founded the earth; by understanding He established the heavens; by His knowledge the depths were broken up, and clouds drop down the dew.**
>
> **(Proverbs 3:19 –20)**

The Lord delights when we take an interest in the mystery of His creation – after all, that is, alongside His Word, a substantial part of how we get to know Him. True scientific study does not undermine God but confirms the Word and creates a reverential awe and delight in Him. Taking in good information is fundamental for healthy development and it is God who ordained the system of learning that happens in life. It is natural in God's design that we learn from each other. It cannot be changed – but we must grasp that if we are not learning good stuff, then we are learning bad stuff. If we think we are not learning anything we are deceived. We are still learning, but we are learning 'nothing'. Learning nothing is death. Now there's a thought.

What injustice did your fathers find in Me,
that they went far from Me and walked after
emptiness and became empty? And they did
not say, 'Where is the Lord...?'

(Jeremiah 2:5–6, NASB)

How long will you slumber, O sluggard?
When will you rise from your sleep? A little
sleep, a little slumber, a little folding of the
hands to sleep – so shall your poverty come on
you like a prowler, and your need like an
armed man.

(Proverbs 6:9–11)

We cannot help learning something from those we
are near. Those who have authority in our lives
teach us the most, good or bad. These are our role
models.

My granny would always say, 'You are as good as
the company you keep.' It was in fact part of the
shocking revelation that led to my conversion. I
realised I had become 'the company not to keep'. I
was absolutely horrified – I couldn't get away from
myself. I had to change! Thank God for Granny and
thank God He is the God of new chances. His

mercies are new each morning (Lamentations 3:23). OK, let's get back to my point.

> **And God is able to make all grace abound toward you, that you, always having all sufficiency in all things, may have an abundance for every good work.**
>
> **(2 Corinthians 9:8)**

A lack of wisdom or poor guidance will lead us to remain under the influence of less able role models, or at worst those who either crush our natural gifts or twist them into destructive forms. This truth is huge, not just for you as an individual, but also for whole populations that remain subject to repressive authorities and poor role models. Each of us must break free of a passive mindset and walk in the light of God's Word. He promises us breakthroughs and victories. He is the victorious King.

I want you to check now; think about the company you keep. Think about those you admire and aspire to. Think about those in authority over you. Go before the Lord and ask Him honestly whose advice you should take. Ask Him to give you revelation to filter the influences in your life.

**Search me, O God, and know my heart; try
me, and know my anxieties; and see if there is
any wicked way in me, and lead me in the way
everlasting.**

(Psalm 139:23–24)

The consequences and effects that role models have
on our lives are huge, but the promises of hope in
God's Word are still greater. I believe that the
drummer who declares this greater hope in praise
and whose beat is filled with the passion of God's
love can be a mighty spiritual surgeon for the work
of God's restorative hand.

**And in every place where the staff of punish-
ment passes, which the Lord lays on him, it
will be with tambourines [*tof*] and harps; and
in battles of brandishing He will fight with it.**

(Isaiah 30:32)

He or she can impart the heart of this message
through striking the drum. It can be a beat that stirs
hope, a rhythmic language that motivates and
brings change. The rhythm can carry the heartbeat
of the Lord as He urges His precious church to rise
to the call of her glorious Bridegroom.

> **Raise a song and strike the timbrel [*tof*], the pleasant harp with the lute. Blow the trumpet at the time of the New Moon, at the full moon, on our solemn feast day. For this is a statute for Israel, a law of the God of Jacob. This He established in Joseph as a testimony, when He went throughout the land of Egypt, where I heard a language I did not understand. 'I removed his shoulder from the burden; his hands were freed from the baskets. You called in trouble, and I delivered you; I answered you in the secret place of thunder.'**
>
> **(Psalm 81:2–7)**

It can be the prophetic sound that speaks of the coming King. Jesus is coming! As I write, I am stirred. I can sense what feels like a rumbling from the deep. It is as if the drumming is joining the rumblings of God's molten lava deep in the heart of the earth. Not literally, but spiritually. . . It is getting ready to explode with the mighty presence of Almighty God.

> **The Mighty One, God the LORD, has spoken and called the earth from the rising of the sun to its going down. Out of Zion, the perfection**

of beauty, God will shine forth. Our God shall come, and shall not keep silent; a fire shall devour before Him, and it shall be very tempestuous all around Him. He shall call to the heavens from above, and to the earth, that He may judge His people: 'Gather My saints together to Me, those who have made a covenant with Me by sacrifice.' Let the heavens declare His righteousness, for God Himself is Judge.

(Psalm 50:1–6)

I want to encourage you in God's Word. Are you catching the excitement of these passages?

Thus says the LORD, your Redeemer, the Holy One of Israel: 'I am the Lord your God, who teaches you to profit, who leads you by the way you should go.'

(Isaiah 48:17)

The amazing thing is God loves you, and regardless of your history, He wants, if you'll let Him, either to start the process of restoration in your life or to deepen it. He wants to transform your concepts and values in music too. He wants to inspire you in your drumming. He wants to reveal what true worship is. He wants to bless you. One way He will do this is to guide you to people whom He wants to influence you: they will be good company for you.

> **'You are My friends if you do whatever I command you . . . I chose you out of the world.'**
>
> **(John 15:14, 19)**

There are many good Christian drummers out there whom we can look to and who can influence our playing and our lives. Yet often, and especially in our climate of celebrity, they can be unapproachable. Why not ask God to help you get connected to someone who can influence you and act as a good role model, both for your playing and your lifestyle? The key will be looking for the opportunity to serve, and in serving you will receive. Other mentors, teachers and role models can be found in writings – especially and most beneficially in the Bible.

There are huge numbers of people recorded in Scripture and perhaps you have been like me in the past and skipped through some of the sections listing genealogies, or passed over names often difficult to say. But each of these names represents someone – a person not unlike you or me, a man or a woman, boy or girl whose life journey figures significantly in God's story, just like you do. Each is included in the Bible to inspire us and for us to learn from. For many years I was distanced from those names that appear everywhere throughout God's Word, until one day I heard a Messianic Jew (Christian Jew) speaking at a weekend conference I was attending. This man was reading from Ezekiel and referring to the prophet's vision. Suddenly I noticed something was different. This Jewish believer was recounting what Ezekiel had seen and done from the perspective of relationship. It was as if he were proudly talking about his Great Uncle Zeke, and because he was a relative there was a special connection with what he said and saw. This was not just an academic study of an ancient work, with some intellectual point to be drawn from it. This was Uncle Zeke's testimony of walking with the Lord! I cannot claim to have got to know all the people of the great biblical family tree I am adopted into, but I am starting to know one or two a little more. Uncle Asaph is for me a special inspiration.

As I started to search the Scriptures for wisdom as a drummer, I first of all came across the prophetess Miriam, who is recorded leading the maidens in song with hand drums [*tof*] in Exodus 15:20, and then the Levite priest and percussionist Asaph, who is first mentioned as the father of Joah in 2 Kings 18:18 and in his own right in 1 Chronicles 6:39. He is interestingly referred to (unlike the others listed) as his brother's right-hand man.

My particular interest in Asaph grew as I discovered the considerable influence he held in King David's court and also that he has twelve psalms attributed to his name (Psalms 50 and 73–83). By the way, it looks like eleven at first, but just count them up again . . . it's good for your drumming too! Three bars of four in total, or perhaps a lead note (Psalm 50) . . . a pause (Psalms 51–72) and then dive in for a bar of two (Psalms 73 and 74), and three bars of three (Psalms 75–83). Get it? I'm just playing around. You can ask me when you see me, OK? Back to our role models now.

What good news for us that God has given us records of two God-fearing percussionists in His Word: the prophetess Miriam and the priest Asaph.

Miriam the drummer

Four out of the seventeen scriptural references for *tof* specify that it was women who were drumming, suggesting that this was a regular social and community activity. Here in Exodus 15:20, at the second biblical reference to *tof*, we meet Miriam the prophetess: 'Then Miriam the prophetess, the sister of Aaron, took the timbrel [*tof*] in her hand; and all the women went out after her with timbrels and with dances.'

Miriam was Moses' and Aaron's sister, born at Amran in Egypt during the slavery years. She clearly had a significant leadership role among the women and stood with Aaron to initiate the Lord's instructions given to Moses for Israel. She became rebellious, questioning Moses' relationship with the Lord in Numbers 12, and was severely rebuked, suffering seven days of intense leprosy as punishment. She did, however, come back to journey on through the wilderness with Israel until she died, being buried at Kadesh shortly before Israel entered the Promised Land. Miriam holds a very significant place as the only named drummer in the Bible. She remains for us a drumming role model who stood in leadership, bringing forth prophetic songs and leading the women in celebration with song and dance.

I am always pleased when I meet women who have a heart to drum for the Lord, and saddened that female drummers are in the minority. I am convinced this is because of the male-dominated music culture of the Western world, and it is especially connected with the aggressive use of the drum set that provides the beat in most contemporary music forms. However, I am also convinced the Lord has not stopped passing out drumming gifts to women; it is simply that there is a resistance to it coming forth. There is the attitude that, along with toy cars, play guns and building bricks, a drum is a good toy for a boy. I don't disagree, but why not also for a girl? Many simply assume drumming is a boy's thing, but that is certainly not the biblical truth. Female drummers play and sound different; their sense of rhythm and feel is quite different from that of males. It is not easy to capture in words, but the sound and rhythm is often beautifully warm and is less striving. It dances, releases and has a sensuality that is feminine. It is different from a man playing. Women carry a special gift in their drumming and we should honour it and encourage it. My daughters love to drum!

Asaph the percussionist

Asaph was a Levite by birth. The Levites were one of Israel's twelve tribes and were appointed to the priestly duties surrounding temple sacrifice and worship. They would therefore have been well acquainted with the finer details and requirements of Israel's statutes in the Torah (the Old Testament law). Asaph was an eminent musician, appointed as chief, and was given great authority to lead and to act as role model among the Levites. He was quite literally a professional prophetic percussionist on the regular staff of the Temple. Quite a unique role and quite a challenge to say – particularly if you try it five times in a row at speed!

As already mentioned, Asaph stands out as being credited with twelve songs recorded in the book of Psalms (Psalms 50 and 73–83). It is through these psalms that we can really get to know Asaph and in turn allow his love and fear of God and his character to influence us today. In getting to know Asaph a little, you will find a man of immense integrity, a faithful and diligent servant of the King, and a musician dedicated and passionate in his love of God. He was given the extraordinary privilege of being asked to minister to the Lord with his cymbals.

And he appointed some of the Levites to minister before the ark of the LORD, to commemorate, to thank, and to praise the LORD God of Israel: *Asaph the chief,* **and next to him Zechariah, then Jeiel, Shemiramoth, Jehiel, Mattithiah, Eliab, Benaiah, and Obed-Edom: Jeiel with stringed instruments and harps, but** *Asaph made music with cymbals.*

(1 Chronicles 16:4–5, italics mine)

This tabernacle ministry is often overlooked in commentaries, but think for a moment: David is ordained by the Lord Almighty as king over all Israel. He is given clear instruction by the Lord in all matters surrounding the tabernacle and has the Mosaic law (*Torah*) to help get it right. There are a number of very specific acts for the priests to follow in preparation and sanctification surrounding the tabernacle – in short this is a pretty top job to be operating in. David commissions Asaph as chief over nine other musicians and singers to minister to God with his cymbals. They are to bless God and make an appropriate and sanctified worshipping sound with cymbals and stringed instruments. This is right in the presence of the most high God. Now, come on, this is not just a little bit of nice atmosphere; it is not some piped ambient vibe to add to the nice interior design of the tent of meeting. This is inspired. This was Asaph's job. I like Asaph.

CHAPTER 5

The Drummer's Psalm

Psalm 81 – a psalm of Asaph

Sing aloud to God our strength;
Make a joyful shout to the God of Jacob.
Raise a song and strike the timbrel,
The pleasant harp with the lute.

Blow the trumpet at the time of the New Moon,
At the full moon, on our solemn feast day.
For this is a statute for Israel,
A law of the God of Jacob.
This He established in Joseph as a testimony,
When he went throughout the land of Egypt,
Where I heard a language I did not
understand.

'I removed his shoulder from the burden;
His hands were freed from the baskets.
You called in trouble, and I delivered you;
I answered you in the secret place of thunder;
I tested you at the waters of Meribah. Selah

'Hear, O My people, and I will admonish you!
O Israel, if you will listen to Me!
There shall be no foreign god among you;
Nor shall you worship any foreign god.
I am the LORD your God,
Who brought you out of the land of Egypt;
Open your mouth wide, and I will fill it.

'But My people would not heed My voice,
And Israel would have none of Me.
So I gave them over to their own stubborn heart,
To walk in their own counsels.

'Oh, that My people would listen to Me,
That Israel would walk in My ways!
I would soon subdue their enemies,
And turn My hand against their adversaries.
The haters of the LORD would pretend
submission to Him,
But their fate would endure forever.

> **He would have fed them also with the finest of wheat;**
> **And with honey from the rock I would have satisfied you.'**

I have taken the liberty of referring to this beautiful psalm of Asaph, Psalm 81, as 'The Drummer's Psalm'. The reason for this is that there is perhaps no greater context or endorsement in holy Scripture for the wholehearted act of praise with drums than this. The call to strike the drum in verse 2 sits amid straight-talking verses that typify the passion of the Psalms and complement the call to honest worship found throughout Scripture. Let's do a little study.

In his book *The Treasury of David* written in the late nineteenth century, Charles Spurgeon wrote of this psalm:

> **The God of the nation, the God of their father Jacob, was extolled in happy music by the Israelites. Let no Christian be silent or slack in praise, for this God is our God. It is regretted that the niceties of modern music singing frighten our congregations from joining lustily in the hymns. For our part we delight**

in full bursts of praise; we would rather discover the ruggedness of a lack of musical training than miss the heartiness of congregational singing. The gentility that lisps the tune in well-bred whispers, or leaves singing to the choir, is a mockery of worship.

On verse 2, Spurgeon writes:

Raise a song. Select a sacred song, and then raise it with your hearty voices. Strike the timbrel. Hit your tambourines, ladies. Let the sound be loud and inspiring. Blow the trumpets and beat the drums. God is not to be served with misery but with happy music. Beat the tambourine as Miriam and the women did at Egypt's dark sea (Exodus 15:20).

The Complete Jewish Bible translation gives us verses 1–5 as follows:

Sing for joy to God our strength! Shout to the God of Ya'akov! Start the music! Beat the drum! Play the sweet lyre and the lute! Sound the shofar at Rosh-Hodesh and at full moon for the pilgrim feast, because this is a law for Isra'el, a ruling of the God of Ya'akov. He

placed it as a testimony in Y'hosef when he went out against the land of Egypt.

Here is a clear call from the chief musician Asaph, under the authority of King David, to gather for wholehearted praise and worship. Let's look a little closer. This is not just a nice idea or a suggestion for when we have all got a little bored and want to let off some steam. This is not a new Israeli trend or the influence of a new fashion for noisy worship that's crossed over from ancient Greece. This is not some slightly 'questionable' fringe of the church! This is instruction coming from the highest musical authority in biblical history. It is they who are encouraging us in this full-on expression of worship.

Sing aloud, blow the trumpet, strike or beat the drum! Are these expressions of a self-contained, mild or 'man-pleasing' nature? Is the drummer gently tapping the drum? No, this is clearly wholehearted praise. This is full on. Asaph is saying, 'Drummer, beat your drum.'

Most important of all, this call to praise is an instruction that comes down from an even higher authority – in fact the highest authority of all. It comes from Him who is the beginning and the end of all authority, the inventor and creator of all that is good; Him who knows all things, the unchanging, all-powerful, most beautiful, utterly and frighteningly awesome Lord God Himself.

Asaph states very boldly in verse 4, 'For this is a statute for Israel, a law of the God of Jacob.' Wow! Sit back, all you critics of 'go for it' praise and worship. The heavyweights are trying to tell us something.

The Holy Spirit has given Asaph a word for the church and a word for the drummer: 'Go for it! Praise Him with all you've got, and you, drummer, strike your drum! Yes, I give you permission . . . hit it hard!' (Paraphrased!)

By the way, the word here referring to 'law' is *Torah*, which is not quite as simple as it might appear in common English. We must be careful not to become legalistic in this, nor fall into condemnation, worrying whether we have 'gone for it' enough! Neither, however, must we dismiss it under the false premise that everything 'lawful' in the Old Testament is finished and therefore to be ignored. This is not 'do it or else' law, but 'do it because I have ordained it' law; and be clear about this: in doing it, you are hitting the mark. I have been told the *Torah* can be appreciated as the right knowledge, guidelines, tools or teaching through which an archer will grow in the skill of hitting the bullseye, not once but every time. It is the Lord's desire that each of us learns how to hit the bullseye through the way we live.

Not only does this psalm affirm the drummer's gift and role in worship, but there is also more to be learned. It is stirring to see there is a rhythmic quality in the timing of events that is the call to worship. Verse 3 reads: 'Blow the trumpet at the time of the New Moon, at the full moon, on our solemn feast day.'

The pattern of following the cycle of new moon, full moon and feast days is important on many levels. It is an ongoing bi-monthly activity (new moon and full moon) that follows, and falls in step with, the timing of creation. It is part of God's rhythmic order in creation. It stands as a reminder that the full moon and its cycles are the Lord's. I might add that it could be to the church's benefit to look more for God's hand in the rhythms of creation and even to celebrate the moon's beauty and relevance in keeping with God's Word. More importantly, though, it is an act of surrender, as the worshippers of ancient times plan to order their lives around the Creator's schedule. In rhythmic terms it becomes a metaphor for playing 'in time', allowing the music to follow the conductor, or the drummer to keep the beat tight with the worship leader. The order and movement of creation has for too long been marginalised in Christian thought and lifestyle. We must also break the pattern and bondage of its association with witchcraft and the demonic. It is a theft that the Lord despises (see Deuteronomy 18:9–12; Isaiah 47:12–14). These rhythmic patterns are of God's design:

> **Then God said, 'Let there be lights in the firmament of the heavens to divide the day from the night; and let them be for signs and seasons, and for days and years.'**
>
> **(Genesis 1:14)**

The timing of these gatherings is not fixed by a calendar of numbers (for example, meeting every other Sunday or Wednesday evening), but by the heartbeat of creation. These moments of wholehearted praise rise in step with God's design, acknowledging His creativity and His beauty. There is surrender to God's timing in gathering to worship in step and within His rhythmic design.

> **The heavens declare the glory of God; and the firmament shows his handiwork. Day unto day utters speech, and night unto night utters knowledge. There is no speech nor language where their voice is not heard. Their line has gone out through all the earth, and their words to the end of the world.**
>
> **(Psalm 19:1–4)**

The rise and fall (full moon and new moon) through the seasons speaks of the consistency of God's rhythmic order. It prophesies His unchanging nature. Perhaps if we were to do more than just respond to the call to worship, and commit to doing it in time with God's creative rhythm, we might enjoy and discover a new blessing. As we surrender control of the rigid structure of our own mini-kingdom, we stand to view the kingdom of God afresh. As we let go of our beat and step in time with God's heartbeat we receive new revelation.

To everything there is a season, a time for every purpose under heaven.

(Ecclesiastes 3:1)

Asaph tells us more, as he states in verse 5 that God established this call to worship through His grace and redemption when He set Israel free from the slavery of Egypt.

This is all to do with the miraculous events of Moses' years leading Israel out of Egypt, and their wilderness journey through to the time of their readiness to enter the Promised Land. It must be important – it takes up a massive sixth of the Old Testament. Perhaps this is in part why the Lord ordained a regular service of remembrance for it – a service with full-on praise and plenty of full-on drumming! The miraculous deliverance and establishment of the nation of Israel is a much-repeated prophetic metaphor that speaks of the work of Christ. It represents our own freedom from slavery, our onward journey of learning to trust and worship the Lord Jesus. It is something the Lord has been trying to 'drum into us' since the time He prompted Asaph to write Psalm 81. Actually, since the very beginning. . .

The words of this psalm again reveal the Lord's amazing patience and love, as He desires to lead His people on to the lands of promise. It is a march that requires a beat; for Israel it was the journey of surrender and obedience in preparation for the glorious Jordan crossing (the second crossing at the end of the wilderness years), when God takes His people into the Promised Land. It is the same for us today; a journey of marching in time with God's plans, His rhythmic order in our communities, our churches and our nations. Can you see the drummer's role in this? Can you see your role in it? Incidentally, the biblical story also bears a warning of the consequences for those who were full of complaint, rebellion and fear – they missed out. They did not cross over into the Promised Land.

> **I am the one who corrects and disciplines everyone I love. Be diligent and turn from your indifference. Look! Here I stand at the door and knock. If you hear me calling and open the door, I will come in, and we will share a meal as friends.**
>
> **(Revelation 3:19–20, NLT)**

The next few verses in Psalm 81 continue by stepping up with even more good news. The chief musician Asaph (are you getting to like him too?) prophesies healing and release in the context of this wholehearted praise:

> **I removed his shoulder from the burden; his hands were freed from the baskets. You called in trouble, and I delivered you; I answered you in the secret place of thunder.**
>
> **(v. 6)**

I have often heard the testimony of Christians who have found the mysterious healing touch of the Lord (both physical and emotional) during a time of musical worship. As a drummer, or indeed any musician or singer, you should never forget the power God releases amid honest praise. The sound of true praise and worship will often dispel the presence of darkness.

While I was hosting the London drum-circle for praise and worship with Psalm Drummers, it was not uncommon to witness signs of God's healing touch. Many times I heard, 'I'm not quite sure what happened, but I feel different. I feel as if something has been lifted from me.'

On one occasion a man became extremely angry and, as we continued to play, started shouting and screaming. Two experienced ministers drew near to pray over him and confirm the Lord's promise of freedom as others continued to drum in worship. Very soon the manifestations finished and the man declared his deliverance and the healing power of Jesus.

More often there were healing tears. Tears released from the hurting reservoirs of unforgiveness, pride, fear and sin.

For thus says the High and Lofty One who inhabits eternity, whose name is Holy: 'I dwell in the high and holy place, with him who has a contrite and humble spirit, to revive the spirit of the humble, and to revive the heart of the contrite ones . . . I have seen his ways, and will heal him; I will also lead him, and restore comforts to him and to his mourners. I create the fruit of the lips: Peace, peace to him who is far off and to him who is near,' says the LORD, 'and I will heal him.'

(Isaiah 57:15,18–19)

We must, must, must hold our focus on the Lord. There will always be the potential and temptation for our drumming, our music and our songs to become self-focused. Experiencing the benefits of God's touch and presence can so very easily become the goal. This is not, and should never become, the motivating factor in raising our song to Jesus. At times we need to stop and check what we're doing. Psalm 81 quickly reminds us in verses 8, 9 and 10 of the first commandment:

> 'Hear, O My people, and I will admonish you! O Israel, if you will listen to Me! There shall be no foreign god among you; nor shall you worship any foreign god. I am the LORD your God, who brought you out of the land of Egypt.'

> And God spoke all these words, saying: 'I am the LORD your God, who brought you out of the land of Egypt, out of the house of bondage. You shall have no other gods before Me.'
>
> (Exodus 20:1–3)

This comes to us out of His great love. He knows that if we do it His way, if we keep our focus on Him, if we remain in surrender, if we speak out and declare His name, His truth and His goodness despite our emotions or circumstances, we will be in a place to receive from Him. He can fulfil His promises, pour out his blessings, release His healing, revelation, hope and all we need. In fact more than we need. The Lord is speaking through Asaph to us; not just to the Israelites all those thousands of years ago, but now, today, to you and me. He says, 'Open your mouth wide, and I will fill it' (v. 10).

We are not to forget that the Lord comes first; we are not to water down His sovereignty or to allow other things to creep into our lives and set themselves up on godless altars. He has given us a rhythm to follow, a beat to march to. It is His Word and it is His heartbeat. It is when we step outside of His rhythm that we step out of His loving arms and become subject to the elements of the enemy's domain. When we choose our own beat, our own tempo, and pipe up our own clever song, the sins of pride, rebellion and independence take over. As we lose the Lord's beat we fall prey to stubborn selfish attitudes that invade like weeds. These weeds are the works of satanic powers and principalities, and they lead to death!

As Balou the bear from Disney's *Jungle Book* cried, 'Get with the beat, Baggy!' The Lord's beat has joy: 'Sing aloud to God our strength; make a joyful shout to the God of Jacob' (Psalm 81:1).

When we turn our back on our loving Father, we are in grave danger of the corruption that is very ready to take hold. Don't forget the consequences for the Israelites in the wilderness, whose rebellion kept them from the Lord's promise. Please don't be like those in verses 11 and 12 who turned away. Note the Lord's parental anguish as He states, 'Oh, that My people would listen to Me.' Hold firm to the Lord and His ways, and He will bless you. That is His desire.

The rest of the psalm affirms His unfailing loving character. Read it and see how He yearns to protect and bless you, and promises to subdue your enemies. The condition is so simple: do it His way; stay in time with the song.

Open your mouth wide for Him – trust Him. From your own perspective, things might be uncomfortable, even bad. You are perhaps pondering this very issue today. You have been asking the Lord to open a door for you, or bless you with an opportunity, and instead you seem stuck in a situation with no sign of breakthrough or change. How can this be good for me?

Years ago, I had been living in the States and had enjoyed a string of good jobs drumming for some pretty notable artists, when almost overnight I was stuck back in England, penniless. US Customs wouldn't renew my visa and there was no obvious path to returning to the work, friends, church or life that I had been involved in! I couldn't see any good in it – but I knew I had to trust God. After a few months out of work someone offered me a job playing on a children's album. It was a real budget-recording job: twenty-four tracks in one day, a long drive and not very much money. But I needed the work. On my way I was grumbling and feeling sorry for myself. My pride was dented and I felt humiliated. 'I'm too good for this. . . Why has God done this to me? I don't want to play on a pesky kids' album!' Then the Lord's spirit convicted me and called me to repent. He spoke to me about His love for children and encouraged me to give my all, to make my offering with a good attitude and to trust Him. Yes, it was a tough day. I continued to wrestle with it, but I determined to do it wholeheartedly and trust God. Little did I know that through that single job, playing on an Ishmael 'Glory Company' tape, God would lead me and connect me with some of my most valued friendships and working contacts of the last twenty years.

Remember the first time you had broccoli? You probably thought your mother was trying to poison you! I did. You might love chocolate, but broccoli is really good for you. Mother knows best and so does Father God. You can trust Him in your situation today. If you will determine to change your attitude and receive what He gives you in faith, then He will open doors; His doors, His way, in His time, but for your good, your eternal good:

> **How wonderful are the good things you keep for those who honour you! Everyone knows how good you are, how securely you protect those who trust you.**
>
> **(Psalm 31:19, GNB)**

In conclusion, Psalm 81 could not be more encouraging for the drummer. Written by the great percussionist Asaph, it clarifies in no uncertain terms that it is good to strike your drum in wholehearted praise. Asaph is a brilliant role model and his faithfulness is exemplary. Through his psalms he shows us the joy of playing in worship, and lays out for us a clear example of a heart seeking after God. He makes plain the issue of sin and is unafraid to appeal for God's justice to reign. He is calling us to worship the Lord Jesus with everything we've got. Go for it! Bring your best to the throne of the almighty Lord God!

▲ Bendir, a common frame drum from North Africa (Chapter 1)

▲ Buffalo drum, played by First Nations Peoples of North America
(picture courtesy of REMO Inc.)

▲ Boys' Brigade snare drum made by O'Reilly's of Dublin

▲ Jalapeno drums, photo from a BBC session

▲ LP tambourine with brass jingles

▲ Malachy bodhran hand-painted with Psalm Drummers
star and heart logo

▲ Common tambourine made in China

▲ Tar, a common small frame drum from the Middle East (picture courtesy of REMO Inc.)

▲ Toforan, a large hybrid frame drum designed by the author, made by David Nuttal of Jalapeno drums

▲ *David's Triumph*, painted by Matteo Rosselli conserved in the Palatine Gallery of Pitti Palace in Florence

◀ Historic portrait of a young dancer with a large frame drum

▲ A First Nations elder from the Klamath tribe playing a buffalo drum

▲ An historic picture showing two people of Eastern origin sitting with a large frame drum

▲ Christian Elliott performing with Psalm Drummers at MerseyFest 2005

▲ Participants at a Psalm Drummers workshop

▲ A Psalm Drummer team at Greenbelt 2004

▲ Psalm Drummers from Southampton at a local event

▲ Jerry Brown teaching drummers at Psalm Drummers 2006 gathering, UK

▲ Drummers at Psalm Drummers 2006 gathering, UK

▲ Tom Gregory leading a workshop at Psalm Drummers 2006 gathering, UK

▲ Terl performing with his Jalapeno hand-made drums

▲ Terl in a recording session with the toforan (a large hybrid frame
drum designed by Terl and made by David Nuttal of Jalapeno drums)

▲ Terl at a workshop session at London School of Theology

▲ Terl in worship

CHAPTER 6

Being a Psalm Drummer

'The Psalm Drummers are pioneers. They show that rhythm is woven into the fabric of our humanity, and when taken up by the Spirit, can be a powerful means of prayer, worship, witness and education in a postmodern culture.'

(Revd Dr Jeremy Begbie, Associate Principal, Ridley Hall, Cambridge, UK)

I started Psalm Drummers in 1995 as a response to a dream I received from the Lord in which He called me to gather His drummers, in His service, in this time. There are several other Christian drumming initiatives I am aware of, and Psalm Drummers is not in competition with them. There is a shared heart throughout the world that recognises the call of God for the drummers. The vision of

Psalm Drummers is to bring glory to the most high God and to join with the Father's heartbeat in heralding His Son, Jesus. With the stirring sound of our drums we shall stand as part of Christ's bride in readiness for Jesus' triumphant return.

> Now I saw heaven opened, and behold, a white horse. And He who sat on him was called Faithful and True, and in righteousness He judges and makes war. His eyes were like a flame of fire, and on His head were many crowns. He had a name written that no one knew except Himself. He was clothed with a robe dipped in blood, and His name is called The Word of God. And the armies in heaven, clothed in fine linen, white and clean, followed Him on white horses. Now out of His mouth goes a sharp sword, that with it He should strike the nations. And He Himself will rule them with a rod of iron. He Himself treads the winepress of the fierceness and wrath of Almighty God. And He has on His robe and on His thigh a name written: KING OF KINGS AND LORD OF LORDS.
>
> (Revelation 19:11–16)

Being a Psalm Drummer is the recognition or heart response that says, 'My drumming is God-given. Lord, let me glorify You through it.' Being a Psalm Drummer is to say, 'Here I am, Lord. Send me' (see Isaiah 6:8). Joining Psalm Drummers is agreeing to align with the vision called 'Psalm Drummers'; a vision to surrender to God's plans. It is not exclusive, but must be sincere. Being a Psalm Drummer is joining a network of Christian drummers who are readying themselves, in the pursuit of God's call, as the Lord Jesus gathers and sends His drummers throughout the world with His heartbeat.

Does this resonate with you?

How Psalm Drummers came about

The vision for Psalm Drummers came through a dream I had in October 1994. I was on tour with a band called Iona and had fallen asleep on the tour bus en route. I dreamt I was standing in a semi-circle with a number of other drummers. We were worshipping and declaring God's kingdom by pounding our drums in a strong unison pattern. It was as if we were on duty and called together for this moment. I was working hard. I could sense the others were too. It was very physical and the sound of the drumming was powerful and relentless. I then recognised there was a song, and as I joined in I realised it was from Psalm 97: 'The Lord reigns; let the earth rejoice' (v.1). It was a repeating refrain with all the sense of the following line in verse 2, 'righteousness and justice are the foundation of His throne', captured within it. I knew I was privileged. I was in awe and at the same time fearful. My head was bowed because the light of God's presence was so bright. Beams of intense light were shooting past us with smoke billowing up all around. Then I saw the word 'PSALM' written in capital letters. When I woke up I was not the same. I was inspired and moved.

Sometime later I was sitting in a meeting in London at my then home church, Holy Trinity Brompton (home of the Alpha course), listening to a guest speaker, Steve Chalke. He was giving an inspired talk on callings and mission, with lots of practical advice. He made the simple point that if you have a gift, a skill, or move in a certain cultural group, then the Lord will use that common language and knowledge. Teachers talk about teaching, skate boarders know all about skate boarding, bankers about finance, ocarina players all about small pots with a few little holes, etc! It's not mysterious. The place of your interests and activities is most likely your greatest sphere of influence and that is most likely where you are called to go on mission. It could be a far-off land, but it is much more likely to be right there on your doorstep.

I was quietly pondering my role as a drummer within the music industry when I believe the Lord spoke: 'It's time to gather the drummers.' I confess I shuddered inside. I didn't really know any other drummers. I was fearful and felt intimidated by the idea of meeting other drummers – I felt insignificant. 'Who am I, Lord?' my heart responded. I then pictured the uncomfortable scenario of being introduced to some strange heavy metal drummer and awkwardly asking, 'So what sticks do you use then?' I swallowed and then said, 'OK, Lord, I'll do whatever You want.'

He showed me this: *For thousands of years the drum has offered a beat for the armies of earthly*

*kingdoms. God's drummer offers a beat that
announces the forces of love coming through Christ the
King.*

I started meeting with a handful of drummers in
London in 1995 and was soon hosting a regular
monthly meeting focused on exploring prayer and
worship through drums. God touched those who
came and we spent many hours drumming together
in prayer and worship. Friendships were formed;
some came regularly, others dipped in and out. The
gathering was sometimes three or four, but more
commonly around a dozen. The Lord showed us
things about His heartbeat. He brought healing to
some, re-envisioned others, and showed us how
rhythm can unify peoples from every kind of
background, creed and colour. The meeting grew
and bore much fruit. Many took inspiration from it
and started meeting with other drummers and with
people wanting to explore creative forms of
worship.

Over the first two or three years it was
predominantly drummers who came, and then, more
and more, prayer intercessors, other musicians,
dancers, painters. . . people searching for something

more than their churches were offering. The homeless came. . . All sorts were there and we regularly saw between thirty and fifty each month gathered in a circle with drums. Sessions would last two hours and more as those present called out to the Lord and worshipped Him with all sorts of creative expression. I hosted this meeting each month at various venues in London from early 1996 to mid 2003.

During this period, news of Psalm Drummers travelled fast and suddenly there were meetings using the name all over the UK, and some in Europe and the USA. I got help from family and friends, and we worked hard emailing and meeting with numerous people from across the world. We had several thousand contacts on our database and an ever-increasing number of enquiries about our activities coming in each week. At this stage the movement and vision of Psalm Drummers was looking very much like an organisation. All the advice was to capture it, organise it and form an overseeing body with a legal structure so that we could build. Not bad advice at all really, but as we pursued this route we simply weren't blessed. The blessings were there in the friendships, in worship times and when we gathered teams for events, but not in establishing an organisation.

In late 2003 I was clear the Lord was showing me that this first seven years had been a learning time – a preparation period – but that now a deeper work would start. It was tough to put things down and in a sense let it go, but as I did, through God's grace much of the burden brought by the 'additional' activities was released. Those who were carrying the true vision remained, but many who were perhaps following other visions under the Psalm Drummers banner moved on. There are still many drummers committed to the vision who meet as friends, some who work together and many who host gatherings around the world in association with Psalm Drummers.

For this reason I bow my knees to the Father of our Lord Jesus Christ, from whom the whole family in heaven and earth is named, that He would grant you, according to the riches of His glory, to be strengthened with might through His spirit in the inner man, that Christ may dwell in your hearts through faith;

that you, being rooted and grounded in love, may be able to comprehend with all the saints what is the width and length and depth and height – to know the love of Christ which passes knowledge; that you may be filled with all the fullness of God.

(Ephesians 3:14–19)

This amazing prayer from Ephesians 3 resonates with the Lord's call upon the drummer: to strike a beat that is revelation of both the awesome power and authority of God and the immeasurable grace of the Father. It is the reflection of a heart that welcomes the prodigal home (Luke 15). This is also the essence of the hope presented in the 'heart and star' symbol that is the Psalm Drummers emblem. It is an image of God's heart that beats with almighty passion, reaching out in love: north, south, east and west across the globe. It is coloured red to symbolise the costly sacrifice of the cross. It represents the love that is described in these verses as being 'the love of Christ that surpasses knowledge'. The Lord's drummer understands something of the power of the beat he, or she, places into the air through the Spirit's anointing.

The Psalm Drummer knows deep in his, or her, spirit that the resonation of a drum that beats in praise of the Lord travels further than the range of the human ear. It is a sound that brings pleasure to the heavenly hosts and terror to the forces of evil. It is a beat that strengthens the church with might 'in the inner man', and announces the final authority of Christ as King.

Are you a Psalm Drummer?

The Psalm Drummer's beat is a prophetic sound; it glorifies God and reminds the devil he is defeated. It is a sound that fills the air with a bold message that declares the authority of Jesus as King. It is the drummers of the church making known the manifold wisdom of God to the principalities and powers in the heavenly places.

To me, who am less than the least of all the saints, this grace was given, that I should preach among the Gentiles the unsearchable riches of Christ, and to make all see what is the fellowship of the mystery, which from the beginning of the ages has been hidden *in God*

who created all things through Jesus Christ; to the intent that now the manifold wisdom of God might be made known by the church to the principalities and powers in the heavenly places.

(Ephesians 3:8–10, italics mine)

The name 'Psalm Drummers' stands as a banner name for the player who recognises all of the above. It is not a members' organisation, but a vision statement captured in two words. It is a label to help identify a true desire to seek God's heart in drumming. Psalm Drummers are accountable to God's Word and spur one another on to stand in faith and obedience to God's ordained authorities, namely the church and her respected Bible-believing leaders.

There is a core team that represents the vision, based largely in the UK, with many other drumming friends who carry the vision throughout the world. Psalm Drummers are players of all ages and playing experience, male and female, professional drummers, percussionists, teachers. Many play in church worship bands, some are drum-circle facilitators, and there are those who host drummers' gatherings. Some present workshops in schools and businesses, in churches and local communities. Is that you too?

From the core team there are a number of skilled players who lead teams of drummers to serve at events and who also go on mission. There is also a performing troupe that heralds the vision by appearing at events and teaching from the growing wealth of resources made available at the Psalm Drummers website: psalmdrummers.org

The Psalm Drummers' vision helps teach drummers to see and know more fully the power and purpose of striking the drum for Christ.

Can I be called a Psalm Drummer?

Remember, joining Psalm Drummers is not something you do by signing a form or paying a subscription. It starts with the response of the heart that says, 'My drumming is God-given. Lord, let me glorify You through it.' It is less about joining and more about being. Being a Psalm Drummer is to say, 'Here I am, Lord. Send me.'

Here is a basic framework of eight attributes that help define a Psalm Drummer:

1. A Psalm Drummer recognises Jesus Christ as Lord and Saviour, and all his or her activities aim to be established in the Christian faith and the Bible.

2. A Psalm Drummer seeks to learn about the power and relevance of rhythm in our world and to remain in God's rhythm and purpose for his or her life.

3. A Psalm Drummer believes that the ability to drum is a valuable gift; he or she seeks to grow in that gift with a responsible attitude.

4. A Psalm Drummer acknowledges drumming as a powerful tool for effecting change.

5. A Psalm Drummer plays drums as a declaration of faith and to express his or her worship of Jesus Christ.

6. A Psalm Drummer uses drumming to promote unity and good relationships, to bridge cultural divides and to communicate God's love to all peoples.

7. A Psalm Drummer aims to serve and encourage the body of Christ (the church).

8. A Psalm Drummer is a Christian drummer or

percussionist who is readying himself or herself, in the pursuit of God's call, as the Lord Jesus gathers and sends His drummers throughout the world with His heartbeat.

I have come to realise over the years that many people would call themselves Christians, but that claiming the title is not in itself enough. We can each of us hold up a level of 'good' behaviour that looks right, and probably is good in many respects, but the test comes when we look at the secret parts of our lives, the parts that only God sees. When things happen that are beyond our control we have to throw ourselves unreservedly onto the ultimate truth of the Word and sovereignty of God. The true Christian and the true Psalm Drummer are one and the same – someone entirely committed to the Lord. You cannot bluff being a Psalm Drummer, because that would also be bluffing being a Christian. Jesus told Nicodemus, 'Most assuredly, I say to you, unless one is born again, he cannot see the kingdom of God' (John 3:3). We must continually feed on God's Word and seek His face to allow the flow of His life and Spirit into our lives. It is then that we are not only born again, but continue to live in the new life we have received. Although for some there may be a 'one-off' event that marks the new life, for many others it is a gradual awakening. Either way, to remain alive in Christ requires a diet of God's Word, worship and submission. The daily submission is putting Jesus first in all things; it is a choice and requires discipline (from the same word as 'disciple'). Psalm Drummers are the Lord's disciples.

In Matt Redman's book, *The Unquenchable Worshipper* (Kingsway, 2001), he has a chapter called 'The Undone Worshipper', citing the moment Isaiah sees God on His throne and recognises his own frailty:

In the year that King Uzziah died, I saw the Lord sitting on a throne, high and lifted up, and the train of His robe filled the temple. Above it stood seraphim; each one had six wings: with two he covered his face, with two he covered his feet, and with two he flew. And one cried to another and said: 'Holy, holy, holy is the LORD of hosts; the whole earth is full of His glory!' And the posts of the door were shaken by the voice of him who cried

out, and the house was filled with smoke. So I said: 'Woe is me, for I am undone! Because I am a man of unclean lips, and I dwell in the midst of a people of unclean lips; for my eyes have seen the King, the LORD of hosts.'

(Isaiah 6:1–6)

Matt describes this meeting as

an altogether different kind of meeting, a holy moment marked out by discomfort and soul-searching. The prophet encounters the Lord Almighty, and is never the same again. He realises God's greatness and, in the light of that, his own weakness: 'Woe is me for I am undone!' Isaiah is broken, stunned and shaken in the presence of God. But this brokenness is not a destructive thing; God is stripping him apart in order to put him back together as a stronger, purer worshipper – a worshipper whose heart-cry is, 'Here I am, send me' (v. 8).

This is the Psalm Drummer's heart. A heart-cry that echoes David's words so often found in the book of Psalms.

Know that the LORD, He is God; it is He who has made us, and not we ourselves; we are His people and the sheep of His pasture. Enter into His gates with thanksgiving, and into His courts with praise. Be thankful to Him, and bless His name. For the Lord is good; His mercy is everlasting, and His truth endures to all generations.

(Psalm 100:3–5)

To connect with other drummers and learn more about being a Psalm Drummer visit psalmdrummers.org and join the mailing list. Take advantage of the resources available to help you grow in all areas of your development as a believer and as a drummer. The main thing in being part of a vision like this is to remember you are not signing up to another club or organisation – you are part of a network by virtue of a shared heart after God. It will be important to seek out others near you whom you can connect with. Real relationship happens in and around the local church community, alongside people you can really get to know, and who can get to know you. The website, teaching and resources serve to feed that heart; your heart.

But above all these things put on love, which is the bond of perfection. And let the peace of God rule in your hearts, to which also you were called in one body; and be thankful. Let the word of Christ dwell in you richly in all wisdom, teaching and admonishing one another in psalms and hymns and spiritual songs, singing with grace in your hearts to the Lord.

(Colossians 3:14–16)

'Psalm Drummers are artistic, creative, original, imaginative, rhythmic, dramatic and inspiring. They are able to help us tune into the melody of heaven – AWESOME.'

J. John, The Philo Trust, UK

The Voice of Drums

James Blades (1901–1999), the popular British percussionist and professor of percussion at London's Royal Academy of Music, was responsible for the sound of the gong at the beginning of the J. Arthur Rank movies. He also created the 'V-for-Victory' Morse code signal that was broadcast by the BBC during World War Two 150 times a day. The recording echoed the 'da-da-da-dum' phrase that begins Beethoven's Fifth Symphony. He was quoted as saying, 'That was the greatest noise I ever made.'

I've heard comments like the following many times:

- 'The drums are just there to hold down a solid rhythm to support the music.'

- 'I've never really thought that drums did more than keep the beat.'
- 'Drumming is a primitive art form.'

These comments are short-sighted: the drummer can bring much more – and not only things that we can see or hear. I believe you can 'speak' with your drums. You can express yourself in clear and tangible ways through the sounds you make with your instruments. You are a creative being, made in the image of God. He speaks through all He has made, and so can you.

> **Hear attentively the thunder of His voice, and the rumbling that comes from His mouth. . . God thunders marvellously with His voice; He does great things which we cannot comprehend.**
>
> **(Job 37:2, 5)**

God's words are heard as a whisper or a shout, a song or a sound. They are heard deep within the heart and audibly in creation. Your drumming can also be a voice through which you speak, and it can follow the example of the way God speaks. This is sometimes called playing prophetically.

> **And I heard a voice from heaven, like the voice of many waters, and like the voice of loud thunder.**
>
> **(Revelation 14:2)**

It is true that God is deeply mysterious and there is so much we don't understand about Him. However, He also makes things plainly simple when we are prepared to open our hearts and search the Scriptures. It is through His Word that we grow in wisdom and understanding, and learn how He communicates.

> **The heavens tell of the glory of God. The skies display His marvellous craftsmanship. Day after day they continue to speak; night after night they make him known. They speak without a sound or a word; their voice is silent in the skies; yet their message has gone out to all the earth, and their words to all the world.**
>
> **(Psalm 19:1–4, NLT)**

Do you remember in Chapter 3 how we saw that God's Word calls us to play with *sakal* – which means with wisdom and insight? *The Cambridge Dictionary* says that 'insight' means '. . .a clear, deep and sometimes sudden understanding of a complicated problem or situation'.

God's Word does not only appear as a spoken language; it is heard in the sounds of creation. Other sounds carry God's voice and your drumming can carry your voice too. It can express the words and intent of your heart. This may seem mysterious, but it needn't be.

There are three very simple ways of viewing this:

1. You can create sounds or rhythmic patterns that have meaning, as in James Blades' Morse message of victory.
2. Your sounds and rhythm can speak through the atmosphere or mood you create with them. For example, in its simplest form, a fast beat speaks of something hurried, and a slow beat something restful.
3. Your sounds and rhythms can carry the language of your heart and become an expression that speaks to the listener's heart. This is the language of wisdom and discernment, which is at work in all our communications. You can learn to bring real meaning to the voice of your drumming. As a

listener you are able to differentiate between a genuine or a fake smile, the motive behind a touch, and the honesty of a song. As a player you can develop clarity in what you are able to express.

The first example is the very practical application of the use of your sounds. It might be as obvious as creating a rhythmic motif in a song. Each time it happens it cues a new passage. The music of church bells uses this form of communication. A community could easily recognise the difference between 'a call to worship' and 'a state of emergency'. You can take a word phrase or short passage of Scripture and turn it into a series of rhythmic phrases. It can prompt the listener to the words and meaning and serve to express your voice. A simple way of seeing this work is to tap out the rhythm of a familiar tune or nursery rhyme for a friend, then ask them if they know what you are saying.

In the second example, you can very easily play and also interpret rhythms and sounds based on the pace and feel of them. Although it is not often spelled out in these terms, it is a very obvious language. Imagine an angry drum pattern: it is loud, intense, 'in your face'. I expect you can easily play it for me. Of course it varies, reflecting all the different ways people can be angry, but you will know what I mean. It's not mysterious at all. The same is true of a peaceful drumbeat. The tempo is slower and is stable and uncluttered. Do you hear it? A march beat is rigid and disciplined, speaking of order and authority, whereas a swung beat or Latin groove speaks of freedom and joy. Think of some other expressions: awe, humour, sadness, chaos. . . It's easy really, isn't it?

This is just the start – simple examples of how you can speak with your drums – but you can go deeper. In the third example, you can bring your natural God-given senses into play. It is something you do all the time as you listen to music, but you can learn to apply it as you play.

The way to do it is to decide what you want to speak, what heartfelt expression you want to bring, and, in faith, go for it. As you practise, it becomes easier and, just like any language, it develops the more you do it. Your discernment and expression develop together.

Using these examples you can play with real focus and intent, causing your 'drumming words' to affect the listener and surroundings.

To the intent that now the manifold wisdom of God might be made known by the church to the principalities and powers in the heavenly places.

(Ephesians 3:10)

Be very clear: as you drum, you can make the manifold wisdom of God known to the principalities and powers in the heavenly places. That is to declare God's sovereignty and the devil's defeat. It is part of God's plan that you do this. You can do this with intent and insight, knowing exactly what you are saying with your drums. It is clear from the Bible that many different activities can act as channels for God's voice and can carry yours too – including your drumming.

Let's look at the mysterious relationship between the *spoken* word and our drumming voice. The Bible is very clear about the importance of the spoken word:

Let the words of my mouth and the meditation of my heart be acceptable in Your sight, O LORD, my strength and my Redeemer.

(Psalm 19:14)

Sing to Him a new song; play skilfully with a shout of joy. For the word of the LORD is right, and all His work is done in truth.

(Psalm 33:3–4)

It is a huge area for study and I would suggest that further reading on this subject is essential (see Suggested Reading at the back of this book). However, our grasp of the domain of sound is so often minuscule. Be in no doubt that when we use the Word of God aright in warfare we are assured of victory: 'For the word of God is living and powerful, and sharper than any two-edged sword...' (Hebrews 4:12).

We are speaking those words in English because our Bible is in English and that is the language we speak. However, if we were French or Chinese we would declare the Word of God in French or Chinese and we are still assured that the Word of God is alive and full of power! The power and authority of the Word of God is a supernatural force *within the sounds* of each language as it speaks the Word!

Jesus never spoke English when He was on the earth, but His recorded words in the Bible, in every language, carry supernatural authority. Without God's Spirit and insight, words are merely rhythmic groupings of sound shapes, drumming is just a beat, a conversation is powerless. The more you think about it, it's really extraordinary. Can you see how this relates to your drumming? I hope this helps you grasp something of the rich language you have available in your drumming. I hope it reveals something of the immense diversity of the language of God.

Can you see how your drumming can carry and express the words of your heart? It can carry God's Word that dwells in you, and through the sounds and rhythms you make, it can speak of the things of God. It is a powerful weapon for pulling down strongholds; it is a powerful language that can unify and encourage. If you play from the heart and purpose to bring forth a language of rhythmic words, you will be a significant voice for the Lord.

Your drumming voice is a precious gift. Guard it, invest in it and treat it well. 'Above everything else, guard your heart; for it is the source of life's consequences' (Proverbs 4:23).

Once a year in Northern Ireland the Orangemen take up their drums to march down the infamous Garvaghy Road. The drumming is the language of provocation and is deliberately aggressive. It causes a huge reaction that is heard in the worldwide media each year. For thousands of years men have used the language of drums to strike fear into an enemy. You can speak the language of love, joy, peace and grace through your drumming – and at the right time also strike fear into the enemy! When your heart is aligned with God, you will communicate the things of God through your drumming. When the Spirit of God falls on you, God can and will do extraordinary things through that language.

Remember God's Word in your heart as you play your drums. Think about what He wants you to say. Express it in the tempo, dynamics and feel of the rhythm. Make your beat speak. Let it speak out the Word of God through you. God's Word has limitless power: 'I am the Alpha and the Omega, the Beginning and the End,' says the Lord (Revelation 1:8). 'In the beginning was the Word, and the Word was with God, and the Word was God' (John 1:1). God is the beginning and end of all things, the one true defining power.

The Lord Jesus urges us to live in His Word; to respond to it, feed on it and hold it dear to our hearts; to express it through all we do – which means through our drumming too:

> **My son, attend to my words; consent and submit to my sayings. Let them not depart from your sight; keep them in the centre of your heart. For they are life to those who find them, healing and health to all their flesh.**
>
> **(Proverbs 4:20–22)**

Alex Acuna (world-renowned drummer and percussionist) said this in an interview with Carlos Benson (director of Drummers for Jesus, USA):

> **One of the greatest men after Jesus was the apostle Paul. When Paul was with the Romans, he spoke like a Roman and when he was with**

the Greeks he spoke Greek and when he was with the Jews he spoke Hebrew. God gave in His Word discernment and wisdom, and He prepared us to be in any place. We are going to continue growing in knowledge of being more like Christ if we continue reading the Word and walking by it, walking by faith, walking by victory! But, if we don't do these things, pray and stay in the Word, then the world becomes a challenge to a Christian because they are not fully equipped. When we are fully equipped by the Word of God there is no challenge. That's why God wants some of us to be in the secular business: so we can be a light, we can be salt, we can make a difference, we can be an inspiration to them – not only musically, but spiritually.

Alex understands that God's Word contains all he needs to go anywhere and everywhere that God sends him. His drumming is full of the language of his heart, which in turn is full of God's Word. That is a big part of how he is salt and light in the secular music industry.

There are three things to recap here:

1. God's Word (the Bible) is the absolute truth – God describes Himself and His Word as one.
2. God's Word is not limited to our common language. He speaks in many languages: in words, in sounds, in creation, in visions and through all He has made.
3. You and I are made in His likeness and communicate in many languages: in words, in sounds, through all we make – including drumming.

A young boy's drumming often speaks of passion and excitement, of determination and a desire to be heard. A mature drummer's language has a depth and certainty about it and can speak dynamically in many rhythms. A woman's drumming often carries the language of compassion. Though passionate it remains sensitive – it is very special. One drummer's language might be peaceful and reassuring, while another's will be intense and authoritative. Each has the opportunity to bring something of worth.

Our duty as 'Sound Creators' means that we constantly encourage, share, and reach out

**to all those curious enough about this
phenomenon.**

(Evelyn Glennie)

I had the honour of acting as the facilitator for
more than 350 men and women drumming together
at a Psalm Drummers gathering in Pennsylvania,
USA, in 2002. At one point I signalled for just the
women to drum. It was fascinating; the heart of the
women brought a sound and voice that was clearly
feminine. It had gentleness to it, but great
determination, and perhaps most noticeably it
danced. It was so stirring. Then when all the boys
and men joined in, the beat became war. It was
thunderous and very powerful. It was not hard to
see why military leaders have used the beat of
drums to march to ever since the dawn of time.
However, it must be noted that within the Scripture
references for drumming it is often the women's
drumming that is recorded, offering a beat and
rhythm of joy and celebration – welcoming home
the armies of the Lord.

Bringing together the understanding of the power
of words and the power of drumming can help give

vision and purpose to your playing. Think about who you are in Christ, who He has made you to be. Are you a peacemaker or a warrior? A leader or faithful support? Are you a stabiliser or a challenger? Do you reflect this well in your drumming and have you learned how to express your heart in the words, phrases and language of your drumming?

Drumming is a language through which you can express your worship. Drumming is not a timid expression. It doesn't have to be loud, but it does have to be confident. Each beat carries its comment. A clear, well-defined beat or a well-pronounced rhythm speaks volumes. Understanding the character of the beat or rhythm can seem mysterious, but it needn't be so. When you apply the biblical principles of language to your playing, it becomes easy to express the language of your heart through the sounds of your instruments.

During the time I worked for the band Iona (1991–1998) we often played a piece called 'Kells'. Within the lyrics it declares:

His Word shall live forever; His Word shall
   live forever.
The word is a sword that pierces the heart,
The truth is the light that cuts through the
   dark of this world.
Nations shall rise, nations shall fall,
Nothing shall stand in the way of the Word.

Joanne Hogg (from the Iona album
The Book of Kells, Open Sky Records,
© 1992 SGO Music Publishing Ltd)

It was a powerful and dramatic piece that I felt
inspired to play with four drumsticks – two in each
hand. I had never done this before, but as I had
sought the Lord for the right expression and feel for
it, I had a clear image of sharing the drumming with
the Lord's angelic forces, and that together we
would be battling in the heavenlies. In my spirit I
sensed that each thunderous beat was a direct hit
against the enemy and as I played I knew I was,
with God's anointing, bringing down evil
strongholds and allowing His great light to
penetrate the darkness – just as the song lyrics
announced.

Some years later I was playing at a party in one of London's private gentlemen's clubs. I had been booked to play with a function band, and although I liked the guys in the band, it was not a particularly desirable event. The room was smoky, the sound wasn't great and the inebriated host kept requesting strange tunes that nobody knew. In truth, I was wondering why on earth I was there. After the second forty-five-minute set I went outside to get some fresh air. It was a relief. The London air was cool and I stood for a while watching the black cabs and the bustle of the city.

A few partygoers were wandering in and out, and then one of them came over to talk to me. She said she thought she knew me from somewhere, but she wasn't sure where. As we spoke she realised that she had seen me playing for Iona once and she remembered in particular the piece where I had played with four drumsticks! In the few minutes that we talked she said how she had seen in her spirit at the time that I was, quite literally, destroying demonic forces as I drummed! I was so encouraged. Here I was, in another time and place, wondering about the value of my gift, and the Lord had engineered this special moment to encourage me and to remind me of His power in and through my drumming. I went back into the party with renewed faith, and worshipped Him amid all the unpleasantness that surrounded me.

Let your drumming become a voice that builds up the church and stands as a light in the world. Let God's Word shape the language of your playing, and always seek His wisdom and revelation to be creative in expressing the fullness of the things He has ordained for you to say. Don't just make a beat; say something that you mean as you play.

As you drum, move in the authority of God's Word to celebrate, to praise, to worship, to prophesy, to speak of freedom and to declare God's sovereignty.

The word of the LORD is right, and all His work is done in truth. He loves righteousness and justice; the earth is full of the goodness of the LORD. By the word of the LORD the heavens were made, and all the host of them by the breath of His mouth. He gathers the waters of the sea together as a heap; He lays up the deep

in storehouses. Let all the earth fear the LORD; let all the inhabitants of the world stand in awe of Him. For He spoke, and it was done; He commanded, and it stood fast.

(Psalm 33:4–9)

Let them praise His name with the dance; let them sing praises to Him with the timbrel and harp.

(Psalm 149:3)

CHAPTER 8

Personal Preparation and Application

The famous black American jazz drummer Warren 'Baby' Dodds (perhaps the most influential drummer of his era) said the following:

> When I was a little fellow in New Orleans, I wanted to be a doctor . . . but I enjoyed every minute of my life drumming. My enjoyment, that I was getting out of music, I was sending through to others. I know that some of my drumming touched a lot of people's hearts. If someone was angry, even with domestic troubles, hanging where I was drumming – drumming with my heart – they'd just forget their troubles and be happy. Even if I'd been a doctor, I couldn't have done any more than that.

The young warrior David is recorded in the first
book of Samuel 16:14–23 using his gift to affect
King Saul's life in a positive way:

> **But the Spirit of the Lord departed from Saul,
> and a distressing spirit from the Lord troubled
> him . . . And so it was, whenever the spirit
> from God was upon Saul, that David would
> take a harp and play it with his hand. Then
> Saul would become refreshed and well, and
> the distressing spirit would depart from him.**

As discussed in Chapter 6, your drumming is much
more than a beat underneath the song. It is
absolutely good and right to enjoy it and have fun
with it, but not at the expense of growing in
understanding and authority with it. You have a gift
that is powerful. However, it is only powerful when
you know what to say and how to say it. This means
preparation, and preparation with God means
surrender. When you can learn to express or speak
things of God through your playing, His way at His
time, there is no limit to the power that is released.
It is a language to express all things from prayer to
light-hearted conversation. This preparation is the
balance of exercise and practice (for developing

your playing skills), and the feeding and nourishment of the truth (God's Word).

Try challenging the language of your drumming as follows:

My drumming ... suffers long and is kind; does not envy; does not parade itself, is not puffed up; does not behave rudely; does not seek its own. As I play I am not provoked, I think no evil; I'll not rejoice in iniquity, but rejoice in the truth; I'll endure all things and drum in love, which never fails.

(Personalised from 1 Corinthians 13:4–8)

Now practise. Can you express the above?

My drumming . . . no longer conforms to this world, but is transformed by the renewing of my mind, so that as I play it may prove what is good, acceptable and perfect in the will of God.

(Personalised from Romans 12:2)

Am I playing from the heart? Am I able to play without trying too hard or needing to impress?

My drumming is ... humble and gentle. I will play with patience, making allowance for others' faults because of Your love.

(Personalised from Ephesians 4:2)

Can I play with authority and assurance – with the Father's heart?

With my drumming . . . I will praise the LORD with my whole heart. I will praise His holy name.

(Personalised from Psalm 103:1)

Now really go for it – let the sounds and rhythms speak of the power and might of our great God, the Lord Almighty!

With my drumming . . . I will declare, 'The LORD is just! He is my rock!'

(Personalised from Psalm 92:15)

The rhythm is stable, incorruptible, immoveable and powerful.

My drumming . . . declares the presence of God, who approaches with the noise of thunder. Fire devours everything in His way, and a great storm rages around Him.

(Personalised from Psalm 50:3)

Need I say more? I think you understand.

The exciting truth is that God's Word gives authority for the drummer to strike the drum (*tof*). Go for it in obedience, with sensitivity, with consideration, with preparation, with power, with a servant heart – and without shame. Let your light shine before men.

> **If then you were raised with Christ, seek those things which are above, where Christ is, sitting at the right hand of God. Set your mind on things above, not on things on the earth.**
>
> **(Colossians 3:1–2)**

> **Let your light so shine before men, that they may see your good works and glorify your Father in heaven.**
>
> **(Matthew 5:16)**

The following statements come from some of my Christian drumming friends. They are there to serve as a simple guide for applying biblical wisdom to your playing.

In praise and worship

Let them praise His name with the dance; let them sing praises to Him with the timbrel [*tof*] and harp.

(Psalm 149:3)

Again I will build you, and you shall be rebuilt, O virgin of Israel! You shall again be adorned with your tambourines [*tof*], and shall go forth in the dances of those who rejoice.

(Jeremiah 31:4)

They have seen Your procession, O God, the procession of my God, my King, into the sanctuary. The singers went before, the players on instruments followed after; among them were the maidens playing timbrels [*tof*]. Bless God in the congregations, the Lord, from the fountain of Israel.

(Psalm 68:24–26)

'Being a musician is a wonderful and powerful thing. As a modern-day minstrel of the Lord, I believe we impact the souls of people and affect the atmosphere as we release spiritual sounds with our hands. When playing praise music we are allowed the privilege of touching the heart of God, as well as leading people into His presence. But it seems to me that His Spirit moves through His minstrels no matter what the setting. Like David in the presence of the Lord or before King Saul, we can play in 'the king's court' (the secular world) or 'the Temple' (in the midst of His people) and the anointing will flow. "I will bless the Lord at all times; His praise shall continually be in my mouth." '

Carl Albrecht, drummer, percussionist and producer,
Nashville, TN, USA

'Drums/percussion are a powerful force in praise and worship. The key for me is allowing the Holy Spirit to enter in and being sensitive to the dynamics of praise.'

Carlos Benson, drummer, teacher, Director of
Drummers for Jesus, Fort Worth, Texas, USA:
www.drummersforjesus.com

'The Levite musicians and their families stayed in the rooms of the Temple and were exempt from other duties because they were responsible for the

work, day and night (see 1 Chronicles 9:33; 6:31).
These are the men David put in charge of the music
in the house of the Lord after the Ark came there to
rest. Most of the time I'll wake up in the morning
and think, "Wow! This is the day that the Lord has
made and He did it just for me. That's how much He
loves me." That alone puts my heart and mind in a
special place to praise and thank the Lord with all
I've got. Psalm 103 says, "Praise the Lord, O my
soul! All my inmost being, praise His name. Praise
the Lord, all His works everywhere in His
dominion. Praise the Lord." Being chosen as a duty
officer of worship means I'm on this all day, every
day, so I forget about how I feel, and think about
who He is.'

Jerry Brown, drummer, percussionist, bass player –
UK sessions and tours, Jamelia, Ms Dynamite,
Courtney Pine and Will Young

'In our little church, Tribe of Los Angeles, I like to
think of myself as a "worship facilitator". We meet
in a circle. There is no proscenium, no "worship
team", no audience. We encourage full participation
by all who worship with us. Similar to a drum
circle, but with a DJ, and elements of electronics;

we all play percussion or hand drums, sing and dance. I compose the music so it has no chord progressions and no set structure. Like all ancient music, each piece is based around one tonal centre, or drone. This allows for not only greater partici-pation, but also almost unlimited freedom to allow the Spirit to lead in worship. It is working very well for us. The music is very energetic, and everyone is usually pretty spent after a worship session.'

David Raven, LA studio drummer and for Norah Jones, Keith Richards, Matt Redman, Steve Taylor, Bobby Womack, Amy Grant, T Bone Burnett, Carole King and many more

In celebration

Then David and all Israel played music before God with all their might, with singing, on harps, on stringed instruments, on tambourines [*tof*], on cymbals, and with trumpets.

(1 Chronicles 13:8)

Then David and all the house of Israel played music before the LORD on all kinds of

instruments of fir wood, on harps, on stringed instruments, on tambourines [*tof*], on sistrums, and on cymbals.

(2 Samuel 6:5)

Then Miriam the prophetess, the sister of Aaron, took the timbrel [*tof*] in her hand; and all the women went out after her with timbrels [*tof*] and with dances.

(Exodus 15:20)

'In 1 Chronicles 13:8 the key phrase for me is "[they] played music before God with all their might". It's important that we approach the music we play for God with passion – though that doesn't necessarily mean hitting everything on the kit as loudly as possible! It has more to do with intensity, and that can apply to every dynamic from a whisper to a roar. Intensity comes from the way we play – the way we hear the music and who we are; and that has a lot to do with our hearts – how we are with Him and how we express that on our instruments.'

Phil Crabbe, drummer, teacher – UK Independent, numerous CCM, mainstream and TV sessions, UK Psalm Drummers core team

'As I play with passion and purpose I connect on a deeper level and flow with the Holy Spirit to make exuberant praise. Whether on the kit or playing hand drums, something rises up from my innermost being in celebration. God is searching the earth for those who truly love Him with a passionate, untethered heart.'

Alun Leppitt, pastor, worship leader and Psalm Drummer UK – co-host of Southampton Psalm Drummers, UK Psalm Drummers core team

'Playing drums is a full-body experience. We get to dance, to sing, to interact and to lead. I have often come away from a gathering being hoarse from shouting, spent from playing but feeling totally elated through the experience of encountering the presence of God in celebration. To not commit every part of my being in celebration of Jesus diminishes the depth of this experience.'

Calum Rees, drummer, percussionist, teacher – Psalm Drummers core team, Vineyard and numerous other UK CCM worship albums, UK

For prophecy

After that you shall come to the hill of God where the Philistine garrison is. And it will happen, when you have come there to the city, that you will meet a group of prophets coming down from the high place with a stringed instrument, a tambourine [*tof*], a flute, and a harp before them; and they will be prophesying. Then the Spirit of the LORD will come upon you, and you will prophesy with them and be turned into another man.

(1 Samuel 10:5–6)

Again I will build you, and you shall be rebuilt, O virgin of Israel! You shall again be adorned with your tambourines [*tof*], and shall go forth in the dances of those who rejoice.

(Jeremiah 31:4)

'Music is a language and has the ability to speak for good or bad into all of life's circumstances. I have the privilege of playing gigs large and small, and to experience the power of music connecting with people in both mainstream and Christian situations. We must realise that as drummers and percussionists we have the ability to effect change through our playing. Like the time in Belfast, Northern Ireland, where as Psalm Drummers we were able to bring together the lambeg and the bodhran (very significant drums in the culture), to speak powerfully of reconciliation over a hurting people. Or at a Psalm Drummers conference in the USA where a lone Native American Indian played his indigenous drum over the conference, communicating the history and pain of his people. It is awesome to realise that we can connect with people in such a way through our playing, but with it comes a great responsibility to be honest, humble and real.'

> *Chip Bailey, pro drummer,*
> *drum circle facilitator,*
> *UK Psalm Drummers core team*

'Throughout history, the drum has been used in battle to let the enemy know, "We're coming," or, should I say, "He's coming." Rather than sneaking in, God boldly sends the musicians before the prophets and warriors, setting the tone for what is to come. It's important for us to realise that we drummers are much more than musicians; we are also prophets and warriors. We not only provide an environment for prophecy and warfare by preceding (even leading) the prophet and warrior, but we also prophesy and do battle through the sounds and rhythms we produce. God sends us first because we are able to break down spiritual walls. We prophesy by hearing and seeing what the Spirit is saying and doing . . . then bring it into the physical realm.'

Bart Elliott, drummer, percussionist,
drum circle facilitator, Nashville, TN, USA

'During a visit to central Tanzania, I found myself in a mud hut church with the local Gogo people. After telling my story of God bringing me back to my inheritance and Irish drum, a new rhythm was created as the local ngoma (drum) and my bodhran brought forth a spontaneous sound. After a fifteen-minute drum prayer a local leader stood up and shouted in a loud voice, "I have a dream, I have a dream." He proceeded to prophesy about the

African drum and how God wanted to restore its place among His people. He finished by remembering that in his heart language (Ha) the word for drum and the word for kingdom is exactly the same.'

Martin Neil, drummer, percussionist, educator and itinerant minister – numerous UK/US worship recordings and currently working with indigenous peoples across Africa, UK Psalm Drummers core team

'For me, the most special and even life-changing experiences were not playing in front of 50,000 people, but the times where I allowed the Holy Spirit to guide me and take over. Moving in the prophetic means becoming an expression of God's heart and mind under the creative direction of the Holy Spirit. Only God can use my playing in such a way that it can penetrate people's hearts and change them completely, as well as change my own heart. Use your drums as an expression of God's love, joy, power and wrath as He directs you.'

Frank van Essen, drummer, percussionist, music arranger, Holland/Iona, Ralph van Manen, CCM and mainstream sessions

For freedom

Sing aloud to God our strength; make a joyful shout to the God of Jacob. Raise a song and strike the timbrel [*tof*], the pleasant harp with the lute.

(Psalm 81:1–2)

Praise Him with the timbrel [*tof*] and dance; praise Him with stringed instruments and flutes.

(Psalm 150:4)

'Every time I complete a session of worshipping from the drums I feel like I've just enjoyed the joy of flying, but my feet never left the pedals. The freedom comes from the anointing of the Holy Spirit. Nothing like it!'

Carlos Benson, drummer, teacher, Director of Drummers for Jesus, Fort Worth, Texas, USA: www.drummersforjesus.com

'For me, freedom in worship comes from discipline; we need to hone our skills as drummers. This requires discipline, but our spiritual lives also need to be in order. I have found it very helpful over the

years to memorise and meditate on the Scriptures –
this gives me an "inner storehouse" of God's Word
to draw on while worshipping on the drums.'

Phil Crabbe

'I believe that ordered rhythm is for our healing. So
often, disordered rhythm is a sign that our bodies
and minds are under unhealthy stresses – notice
your breathing, your heartbeat and your sleep
patterns. Playing rhythm or feeling the rhythm that
others play can help restore the rhythms that
support healthy life. As a Christian musician, I am
sure that God means us to play with a healing
intention. If I am aware that someone in the
congregation is labouring under a heavy burden, I
ask God to direct my playing to be a special blessing
to that person.'

*Phil Manning, percussionist, UK, director of Beat's
Thinking and facilitator of corporate rhythm events,
Psalm Drummers core team*

'In the early 90s, in Canada, I found myself
improvising on a Pacific Island log drum.
Unbeknown to me, three large Samoan men on a
year's study course were in the audience, and

approached me after the evening's event with tears in their eyes. In their culture, a log drum is given at birth to males, representing life. Their instruments brought from home had stayed wrapped in cloth at the bottom of their luggage, as they had been taught that their drum was unacceptable in church. On hearing the log drum, God spoke to each one about His love for their people and gave them a wonderful sense of freedom to be who they have been called to be and beat their drums. Later I found out that there is a large log drum in Samoa called the logo and it is known as "the voice of God".'

Martin Neil

In declaration

For through the voice of the LORD Assyria will be beaten down, as He strikes with the rod. And in every place where the staff of punishment passes, which the LORD lays on him, it will be with tambourines [*tof*] and harps; and in battles of brandishing He will fight with it.

(Isaiah 30:31–32)

Now it had happened as they were coming home, when David was returning from the slaughter of the Philistine, that the women had come out of all the cities of Israel, singing and dancing, to meet King Saul, with tambourines [*tof*], with joy, and with musical instruments.

(1 Samuel 18:6)

'There is an absolute freedom when I minister on the drums. My drum set is a weapon and whether I'm on stage in a concert or in a church I'm always on the battlefield (Psalm 144:1). I'm fighting for my own soul and the souls of everyone around me. When David played the harp, Saul's evil spirits fled (1 Samuel 16:23), so whenever I play the drums in the name of Jesus I believe the same is going to happen today, tomorrow and in the days to come. I always pray that whenever I hit my crash cymbal, walls will crash down that stand between an individual and the presence of God. Whenever I kick my kick drum, Satan and his evil plans are kicked away, and whenever I play my ride cymbal, someone rides to victory. AMEN!'

Louis Santiago Jr, drummer, clinician /Jeff Deyo, 2003
Modern Drummer magazine winner

'It's interesting to note that the same instruments are used in anger and in celebration. For me the beauty of percussion is its versatility. There are so many colours to paint with, and they can all be used in worship. I remember once at Spring Harvest using the mark tree (brass wind chimes) to illustrate the line "to weep with your tears" in Graham Kendrick's song "Soften my heart". A lady came up to me afterwards and told me how that sound had helped her to realise that Jesus wept for her. It is humbling when God takes a simple percussion effect and speaks through it.'

Richard Hubbard MA, teacher of timpani and percussion, director of Music & Worship Foundation and Cantus Firmus Trust, lecturer in music at London School of Theology

'Drumming is not a formula; it's about heart and passion. Without these two qualities all the skill in the world leaves the listener empty and unmoved. I believe it is our job as spiritual drummers to bring life to the simplest of grooves and beats, almost as if we were playing the heartbeat of God, bringing life to those that have ears to hear. I have never classed myself as a technical drummer – my style rather resembles that of a slightly out-of-control child after a bag full of blue Smarties. For me there really is nothing like playing before people, feeling God and somehow allowing an audience to be a part of "the journey". The Bible talks a lot about the injustice in our world; I for one want to strike the drum and believe it's possible to be a warrior sounding out a rhythm against injustice and pain and bringing justice and joy.'

Stew Smith, drummer, UK, Delirious?,
Psalm Drummers core team

In disregard of God – a warning

They sing to the tambourine [*tof*] and harp, and rejoice to the sound of the flute.

(Job 21:12)

Woe to those who rise early in the morning, that they may follow intoxicating drink; who continue until night, till wine inflames them! The harp and the strings, the tambourine [*tof*] and flute, and wine are in their feasts; but they do not regard the work of the LORD, nor consider the operation of His hands.

(Isaiah 5:11–12)

The earth is also defiled under its inhabitants, because they have transgressed the laws, changed the ordinance, broken the everlasting covenant. Therefore the curse has devoured the earth, and those who dwell in it are desolate. Therefore the inhabitants of the earth are burned, and few men are left. The new wine fails, the vine languishes, all the merry-hearted sigh. The mirth of the tambourine [*tof*] ceases, the noise of the jubilant ends, the joy of the harp ceases.

(Isaiah 24:5–8)

You were in Eden, the garden of God; every precious stone was your covering: the sardius, topaz, and diamond, beryl, onyx, and jasper, sapphire, turquoise, and emerald with gold. The workmanship of your timbrels [*tof*] and pipes was prepared for you on the day you were created.

(Ezekiel 28:13)

'It is very fulfilling to work in the music industry as a drummer and percussionist. The industry needs Christians not to judge, but to work alongside and love creative people, who are often very vulnerable. Sadly our industry is littered with casualties and as Christians we are wise to have in place support networks of people we trust.'

Chip Bailey

'I think the key things here are integrity and purity. One of the main stumbling blocks for many musicians is pride and ego. It was Satan's downfall, and we need to be wary of it rising in our hearts. We must ask the Holy Spirit to reveal our weaknesses and help us to "take every thought captive to the obedience of Christ".'

Phil Crabbe

'Musically, the percussionist is in a position of power. Whether as timpanist in an orchestra or as drummer in a worship band, we can make or mar the music with the sheer volume of sound we have at the ends of our sticks. That power needs to be harnessed by a servant heart that's committed to a love for God and a lifestyle of worship. When those things are in place, the Holy Spirit can use our skills to point the hearer to God. What would you prefer?

That people comment on your stunning playing, or that they encounter the living God through it?'

Richard Hubbard MA

'It can be easy for music to become an idol or a distraction and for pride to rise up to taint our pure worship. Staying true to what God has put in your heart and remaining humble are vital for any musician. There is also a very real demand on those who are worship musicians to live a life worthy of the calling as we serve a holy God. This isn't about status or position; it's about obedience and heart attitude. Out of the overflow of our heart we speak, so what is in there comes out when we play too – so guard your heart!'

Alun Leppitt

'I believe that we are a people called first to "be" followers of God but often we are more focused on what we "do" for God. Rather than serving, encouraging and building people and community, music in the West can be, at worst, very self-focused. Amos's rebuke has always kept me asking the questions: "Away with the noise of your songs but let justice roll on like a river." '

Martin Neil

'It's not about the gigs or the CDs or the fantastic performances I get to be part of. They all get bolted on to my total dependence on Jesus. As soon as I start playing for playing's sake, forgetting about the context in which I get to play, forgetting about the poor, destitute and oppressed, I can easily become a "professional worshipper" and leave my faith at the door. It's at times like this that I remember the warning of becoming only a "clanging bell" rather than an ambassador for God. The opportunities to play mean nothing without knowing why I'm doing it. It is only through my dependence on Jesus that I will really be alive and free to be how God sees me.'

Calum Rees

'It's sad to see how many wonderful musicians we have lost to the evil in the world. Some say their faith is separate from their business, not realising their gift is a blessing from God. Brothers and sisters, we were given these anointed talents to carry and speak the word of God to those who are lost and needing in the "business"! Do not be ashamed of God!'

Louis Santiago Jr

'Although we all need to be encouraged in our playing and need to encourage others, we have to be careful not to become our own greatest admirers, as Lucifer became. I always try to thankfully accept people's praises, but then redirect them to the One who deserves ALL praise and honour. Pride and self-centredness are among our greatest enemies – a pitfall especially for successful artists! True humility honours God and will, in the end, be your best promoter.'

Frank van Essen

CHAPTER 9

Getting Out There

Ibelieve our calling (drummers, non-drummers, all of us) in the broadest sense can be captured in a very simple vision:

1. To love God with all we've got.
2. To love His church (yes, despite the way she behaves).
3. To go and love the world (totally, despite the way they behave).

For God so loved the world that He gave His only begotten Son, that whoever believes in Him should not perish but have everlasting life. For God did not send His Son into the world to condemn the world, but that the world through Him might be saved.

(John 3:16–17)

Drummers (particularly drum-set players) are often depicted as an aggressive breed. It's not uncommon for a drumming magazine's cover to portray the drummer with a snarling face and clenched fist. There are of course a number of tragic drummers whose outrageous and rebellious behaviour cost them everything, including their lives. Their stories fascinate us and it is an unfortunate human characteristic that our interest is drawn to shocking events and behaviour. The mixed message of skilful playing and an out-of-control lifestyle leaves us (particularly the young) to disentangle what is actually good. The media trade on this all the time, following closely and celebrating the bizarre twins of dysfunction and brilliance mixed together. It is big money! Sadly the dysfunction gets presented as an essential part of the gift. It has influenced many drummers to the point of their own destruction too. It perpetuates the tragedy. It is not the truth.

As I have travelled the world and met numerous drummers from all walks of life, I have found something quite different. Most drummers actually have a gentle nature and self-effacing character.

This is far more impressive in reality – and you and I can model something different to the young people who might otherwise be impressed by the shallow stories that make the news.

Please pray for the gifted musicians who grace the secular world stage – it's a very dangerous place.

For this reason we also, since the day we heard it, do not cease to pray for you, and to ask that you may be filled with the knowledge of His will in all wisdom and spiritual understanding; that you may walk worthy of the Lord, fully pleasing Him, being fruitful in every good work and increasing in the knowledge of God; strengthened with all might, according to His glorious power, for all patience and longsuffering with joy; giving thanks to the Father who has qualified us to be partakers of the inheritance of the saints in the light.

(Colossians 1:9–12)

Going back now to that gentleness I was commenting on before – isn't it just like God to give the weighty responsibility of creating the thunder in the music to the more sensitive personality?

> **But God has chosen the foolish things of the world to put to shame the wise, and God has chosen the weak things of the world to put to shame the things which are mighty.**
>
> **(1 Corinthians 1:27)**

The truth is, we must be unashamed of being who we really are, rising out of 'insignificance' and wanting approval, but not drawn into 'rebellion' to suit the spirit of the world that surrounds us. If you recognise either of these, confess them as sin, receive God's forgiveness and walk in the opposite spirit of significance and humility.

We must take hold of God's Word and rise to His calling on our lives. We must be unafraid to walk in the fruits of the Spirit: love, joy, peace, patience, kindness, goodness, faithfulness, gentleness and self-control (Galatians 5:22–23). Our emotions and feelings must learn to bow before God's Word – otherwise under pressure they will direct us away into stormy waters.

We must be unafraid to lay down the right beat at the right time, God's heartbeat. God's drummer must focus, and hold down the tempo with an uncompromising beat. You can learn to give a beat that carries power and authority under the leadership of the greatest worship leader of all, King Jesus.

Many walk through life hearing about the empowering Word of God, yet fail to respond. Don't remain in passivity. It was prophesied in Deuteronomy 28 (look it up) that when you choose God's way you choose life and blessings. This one step of courage is followed by an enormous list of blessings. Shake off the shackles of unbelief. God's Word promises that you will be made 'the head and not the tail'. In other words, you will rise above, to be on top of events and circumstances and not under – regardless of what they might look like at the time!

> **Do not fear, nor be afraid; have I not told you from that time, and declared it? You are My witnesses. Is there a God besides Me? Indeed there is no other Rock.**
>
> **(Isaiah 44:8)**

The key to the freedom promised in Christ is repentance. If as you are reading this you recognise an area of your activity and lifestyle that is not in line with God's Word, call it what it is: 'sin'. Confess your sin, ask for forgiveness and choose to walk in the opposite spirit. We have all been sinned against, and we must forgive those who have sinned against us, but we have also sinned in the way we have reacted to those who have hurt us. It is a common failing to justify these reactions, particularly when we have been badly hurt. But remember Jesus covered ALL sin at the cross. We cannot punish people for what they have done to us; it will end up destroying us. We must hand the judgement to God and let Him deal with it. We may have become bitter, controlling, full of self-pity, angry, passive, judgemental, envious, rebellious. . . I don't really need to carry on; these reactions are common to us all.

Pray with me:

Lord Jesus Christ, I've sinned against You by being . . . [fill in the blank – it might be a list]. Please forgive me. I truly repent and through the promise of Your Word I receive Your forgiveness. I now also receive the inspiration to do things differently and to walk in the opposite spirit. Help me do this. I will resist the devil and the temptation to continue in this sin, and as Jesus spoke, I now speak to the powers and principalities concerned. I say, 'The Lord rebuke you, spirit of . . .' [fill in the blank: for example, fear, anger, poverty, self-pity, pride, rebellion, etc].

Be firm. Say, 'In Jesus' name, be gone!' You have authority (see 2 Corinthians 10:4–5; James 4:7; Luke 10:19).

With reference to the power of evil in the world:

You are of God, little children, and have overcome them, because He [Christ] who is in you is greater than he who is in the world.

(1 John 4:4)

God is restoring the drum to the church (in praise and worship and more) and is calling drummers, both individually and corporately, to drum out a new beat – a heartbeat that carries the inspiration of the Holy Spirit. The purpose is to declare the Lord's presence. Drumming is a powerful voice for prayer and praise; it can unify the divided, encourage the disheartened and stir up much needed courage within the church in our times.

If you love drumming and sense God's heart for you to do it, invest in it. Ask the Lord to guide you and inspire you to learn. Start practising, get a good teacher, watch videos and listen to other drummers. There are many great drummers who have prepared books and study guides to help you develop your language and technique. Pray for wisdom and spiritual insight alongside your practical development, so that God can shape and direct your path in it.

Delight yourself also in the LORD, and He shall give you the desires of your heart.

(Psalm 37:4)

You will show me the path of life; in Your presence is fullness of joy; at Your right hand are pleasures for evermore.

(Psalm 16:11)

Study Asaph's psalms: he stands out as a role model for Christian drummers and percussionists. He understood his authority in the Lord, he confessed his weaknesses, he applied himself to seeking after God's presence. Asaph was unafraid of judgement, because he knew God loved him.

He wrote, 'I was so foolish and ignorant; I was like a beast before You. Nevertheless I am continually with You; You hold me by my right hand. You will guide me with Your counsel, and afterwards receive me to glory' (Psalm 73:22–24).

Let us take up His call and go His way. We cannot be double-minded about it; we cannot do it in part: we either walk the walk or turn away. The good news is that if we choose the Lord's way He promises victory. If we will be strong and courageous and obey His Word, He assures us of His many blessings and says He will never leave us:

> **Don't be obsessed with getting more material things. Be relaxed with what you have. Since God assured us, 'I'll never let you down, never walk off and leave you.'**
>
> **(Hebrews 13:5, *The Message*)**

> **'I am the LORD your God, who teaches you to profit, who leads you by the way you should go.'**
>
> **(Isaiah 48:17)**

Go with God. Go for it!

> **Give it everything you have, heart and soul. Make sure you carry out The Revelation that**

Moses commanded you, every bit of it. Don't get off track, either left or right, so as to make sure you get to where you're going. And don't for a minute let this Book of The Revelation be out of mind. Ponder and meditate on it day and night, making sure you practise everything written in it. Then you'll get where you're going; then you'll succeed. Haven't I commanded you? Strength! Courage! Don't be timid; don't get discouraged. God, your God, is with you every step you take. ('The Taking of the Land', Joshua 1:7–9, *The Message*)

Playing drums in the world

Over the years I have been asked many times about playing drums in the world or in secular music. As I said before, I believe we all, regardless of gifts, are called to be involved with and serve the church, and also to go out (far or near) and bring God's love as revealed in the Great Commission: 'Go therefore and make disciples of all the nations, baptizing them in the name of the Father and of the Son and of the Holy Spirit' (Matthew 28:19).

It is naturally unwise to go off into the world as a musician without the Lord's permission and direction. You will also need good advice, support, mentoring and prayer cover, otherwise you will be vulnerable to the temptations of seeking fame and fortune on the world's terms. The lure and distractions of the enemy are very subtle and have been refined over thousands of years! You cannot do it in your own strength. When you are called to go, you must get equipped.

It is also just as short-sighted to join the church music team simply because you can play. You will inevitably bring compromising values into the praise and worship, which in turn will undermine the standards that need to be in place in this crucial area of the life of the church.

Each of us, through living in God's Word, in good accountability and with healthy mentoring, will find the right course: 'Show me Your ways, O LORD; teach me Your paths. Lead me in Your truth and teach me, for You are the God of my salvation; on You I wait all the day . . . Who is the man that fears the LORD? Him shall He teach in the way He chooses' (Psalm 25:4–5, 12).

I believe the fully equipped man or woman of God should be both serving the church and reaching out into the world using their gifts and resources to build the kingdom of God. *Obedience is key*. Jesus Himself modelled this for us when He said:

> **'Most assuredly, I say to you, the Son can do nothing of Himself, but what He sees the Father do; for whatever He does, the Son also does in like manner. For the Father loves the Son, and shows Him all things that He Himself does.'**
>
> **(John 5:19–20)**

> **'He who is not with Me is against Me, and He who does not gather with Me scatters abroad.'**
>
> **(Matthew 12:30)**

What about ungodly lyrics?

Over many years I have been asked, 'But Terl, how can you play music that seems to promote ungodly values or has lyrics that serve the kingdom of darkness?'

There are many things to consider in this question. It is never straightforward. I do not endorse a policy to play anything with anybody. However, as I was saying before, it is less to do with the music and lyrics of a performer because if they are in the world, their expression will be of the world. Instead it is all about what the Lord tells you to do, or not to do.

Those who don't know God are quite likely to use a language, say or sing things that are offensive. Expecting something different is unwise. Christians cannot hope for the world to become nicer to suit them.

By getting alongside someone who is offensive, you are not necessarily endorsing his or her offensive behaviour. By drumming in a band you are not necessarily endorsing the music or lyrics either. However, this is such a sensitive and dangerous place to be that you must be completely certain you are in the Lord's will and obedient to His every direction. Get wise counsel, listen to the Lord's voice and be obedient to His Word.

You must understand too that when you play

music with non-believers you will almost always fall into judgement from those who look on. In the same way Jesus was quickly accused of associating with sinners, prostitutes and tax collectors, you will be accused of associating with those Jesus calls you to get alongside.

Remember, Jesus loved you long before you started to honour Him with your mouth or your lifestyle. Unless believers are prepared to mix with those in the world, how will they be reached? The first thing to do must be to ask the Lord, 'Is this something You, Lord, have laid before me to do? What do You, Lord, want me to do?'

This is exercising real faith because it may not always look good from the outside. Beware of the temptations – an opportunity of playing music with someone of notoriety can confuse the heart. Do you want to bring the love of God, or do you actually just want to taste worldly success? Be honest with yourself. Remember too it is likely you will be an employee and not able to change aspects of the environment. Ask the advice of, and pray together with, one or two people you trust. Read how Joseph operated in Egypt in Genesis chapter 39 onwards;

also Daniel in Babylon and the story of Esther. There are many Bible stories of men and women who were positioned alongside and under ungodly rulers and authorities. Each in turn, through obedience to God, brought God's will into the situation.

Seek the Lord's voice. He could say any number of things to you about it. Don't also assume when you are asked to do a Christian or charitable event that it is right to do that either. We should always, like Jesus, seek to do the things the Father tells us to do. If you trust Him and walk in obedience you will not be disappointed. He has your best interests at heart. He loves you.

> **The LORD is my light and my salvation; whom shall I fear? The LORD is the strength of my life; of whom shall I be afraid? . . . Teach me Your way, O LORD, and lead me in a smooth path, because of my enemies . . . Wait on the LORD; be of good courage, and He shall strengthen your heart: wait, I say, on the LORD!**
>
> **(Psalm 27:1,11, 14)**

CHAPTER 10

Practical Insights

Your drums don't make you a drummer.
You are the drummer

It is up to you to grow as a drummer. Your instrument(s) should serve your creative language, not shape it. Too many drummers end up restricted by their own set-up. An impressive drum set is often used to bolster low self-esteem. Don't get trapped – be able to make rhythm with anything, anywhere, anytime. It's good fun too!

Search your heart. Ask: 'Am I bringing anything unhealthy with me?'

It's all too easy to bring distracting baggage with you. Ask God's Spirit to reveal anything that needs dealing with. Perhaps it's very obvious: do you need to forgive somebody or receive the Lord's peace in a situation? Stop playing for a moment and sort it out first. If you are in the middle of playing, ask for God's grace, trust in it and sort things out as soon as you can.

Be in authority as you play

It's all too easy to get distracted, intimidated and undermined, resulting in a compromised performance. Play within your skill range: a simple, stable beat is often the best thing you can bring. Remember, music is a gift from the Lord; rise up in the responsibility of it. Decide to serve well. If you have undermining feelings, deal with them. Memorise some scriptures that you can use to combat the lies. Remember, everyone gets bad feelings: don't let the feelings overrule the truth! The truth is, God loves you, He is with you and His plans are to prosper you. In other words He is all for you (Jeremiah 29:11). If you stand on the truth, you will find freedom (John 8:32).

Be true to yourself as you play

Each of us is made in the image of God and we are all different. God has been so creative in making you. You are not like the rest. We each have different personalities with different qualities and are made to be a blessing to the Lord and those around us. It's no good trying to be someone you're not. Ask God, 'Show me who You have made me to be, Lord.' Let Him affirm your strengths and identity in Him – and let those qualities shape the sound and feel of your beat. Know that you have a voice in your music and it is good and right that you should express it.

Play wholeheartedly, but with integrity

A bored-looking drummer playing a heartless beat may as well go home and watch the television. Remember, God has put rhythm in everything that is alive. Bring your drumming to life – decide that it should always stimulate and lift the music, but never override the other parts. There will always be moments for you to shine forth and release some 'extra' fire, but never play in a threatening manner or with timidity; both hinder the goal of making good music; both are rebellion.

There is always an appropriate thing to do, even if it means remaining silent

Most of the time an appropriate beat or rhythm will be obvious. But when it isn't, try listening to the rhythm of the words or melody. Do they indicate a rhythm? If not, don't force it. Try exploring the use of sound effects instead, such as cymbal swells, drum rolls and non-rhythmic sounds. Do they help? If not, it's time to remain quiet.

Always make music with your drumming

It's a simple thing to say, but as you play either on your own or in a group setting, ask yourself, 'Am I making music?' It is not difficult to get distracted or become overly self-orientated as you play. Of course you should concentrate, but not just on yourself. Maybe you are trying too hard – simplify and join in the wider conversation. Making music is one of the greatest gifts of all. Music is catching, uplifting, exciting; joyful music is a powerful tool that ministers life to the listener. There is a right kind of music for every occasion. Ask God, 'Am I making the right kind of music today?'

Don't warm up at full volume

Drummers and percussionists can be very annoying, endlessly tapping and making distracting noises. It is a common habit and everyone does it, but it is well worth remaining aware of how irritating it can be. Keep a silent practice pad with your set up so you can warm up without causing frustration to others. It is a good way of getting round the problem. Have the courtesy to wait with patience, or perhaps take your instrument or practice pad to another room if you need to.

Enjoy practising

Find creative ways to practise, making it musical and fun. Set aside time to play for fun. You can also use practise to meditate on God's Word, for prayer and worship. Start with a prayer and passage of Scripture and practise for the Lord. Remember, listening is a crucial part of learning: include a diet of listening to music that will challenge you and widen your skill.

Enjoy drumming

I always tell people I love drumming. No, the feeling isn't always there, but the feeling is not the truth. God has so often given me such joy beating the drums – what could be better? Always remember: 'This is the day the LORD has made; we will rejoice and be glad in it' (Psalm 118:24). I have learned and I am learning – it's ongoing. This is God's day; I choose to have a good attitude in it. A good attitude is a choice and it means bringing a good attitude into all you do as an act of worship. 'I will be glad' is having a good attitude. A good attitude honours the truth that God is always good. A good attitude is powerful spiritual warfare and will often break the enemy's fortresses.

CHAPTER 11

Prayer

A drummer's prayer

Dear Jesus, Mighty Lord and King of all,
You are the creator of rhythm.
In You there is no shadow or turning [James 1:17].
You are the same yesterday, today and always
[Hebrews 13:8].
Help me catch Your rhythm afresh today.
Forgive me for striving and trying to steer Your
beat.
I choose Your way for my life. I choose to rest in
Your timing again.
Be the director of my heart and its rhythm now
and always.

Create in me a clean heart and renew a steadfast
spirit within me [Psalm 51:10].
I draw near to You, lay down my plans, my
hopes and fears to listen to Your heartbeat again
[James 4:8].
Bless me with revelation and wisdom to develop
my gifts in You [Proverbs 3:13].
Bless my hands and sense of rhythm with a
prophetic anointing.
Bless me with creativity to play with great skill
and insight [*sakal*].
Release joy and passion into the language of my
drumming.
Be the Lord of my every beat, for the glory of
Your name,
that I might strike the drum, and mark out a
right rhythm each time I play [Psalm 81:2].
May my drumming serve You as part of my
worship,
and serve Your plans for the building of Your
kingdom on earth.
Amen.

A fresh start

As you have read through this material it may be you have been inspired to call out to God perhaps for the first time – or to renew your commitment to follow Jesus as a real disciple. If so, you might like to pray the following prayer. Go for it. . . ALL His promises are true and He will never let you down!

Prayer

'I come to You, Lord Jesus. I want to know You and know Your leading in my life. I have done things I know are wrong and genuinely confess my sins before You [Psalm 51:1–5]. Please forgive me and show me Your grace. I receive Your forgiveness; help me know I am forgiven. The Bible says, 'Whoever calls on the name of the Lord shall be saved' [Acts 2:21], so I call on You now to save me. I recognise that You made me, You created me. I put my hope in You [Psalm 119:73–74]. The Bible says that You love me and will guide me [Psalms 86:13 and 23:1–3]. Please fill me with Your Holy Spirit [Luke 11:13] and start to renew my mind [Hebrews 12:2] so I will know Your will for my life and follow Your commands. I thank and praise You, O Lord.'

You have just done something truly amazing. The Bible says: 'If you confess with your mouth that Jesus is Lord and believe in your heart that God raised Him from the dead, you WILL be saved. For it is by believing in your heart that you are made right with God, and it is by confessing with your mouth that you are saved.' As the Scriptures also tell us, 'Anyone who believes in Him will not be disappointed' (Romans 10:9–12). The Bible also says that God inhabits the praises of His people (Psalm 22:3). Reading Psalm 103:1–6 out loud is a great way to get started in praise. Faith comes from being filled with God's Word. The Bible states: 'The Word was with God, and the Word was God' (John 1:1). The Bible is God's Word (2 Timothy 3:16), so get stuck in: the Gospel of John makes a good place to begin. You also need to connect with, and get alongside, other true believers. This will help protect the seeds that were planted today. I encourage you to join a local church that boldly preaches God's Word and obeys it. Perhaps go on an Alpha course, and seek only God's answers to the questions in your life. For a list of churches running Alpha around the world visit http://alphacourse.org/

May God bless you.

Suggested Reading and Resources

Books

- The Bible, of course! I recommend The New Living and The Amplified versions.
- James Blades, *Percussion Instruments and Their History*
- Geoff Nicholls, *The Drum Book*
- Study/method materials – Gary Chaffee, Joe Morello, Ted Reed, etc. There are many to choose from, but also watch good DVDs. Have a look at Gregg Bissonette, John Blackwell, Chris Coleman, *Hand2Hand* (from Psalm Drummers). Bill Bachmann too.
- Charles Spurgeon, *The Treasury of David*
- Matt Redman, *The Unquenchable Worshipper*
- John Eldridge, *Wild at Heart*
- Joyce Meyer, *Battlefield of the Mind*
- Joyce Meyer, *The Secret Power of Speaking God's Word*
- Kenneth Copeland, *The Force of Faith*

Websites

- Bible study: www.crosswalk.com
- Psalm Drummers: www.psalmdrummers.org
- Terl Bryant: www.voiceofdrums.com
- Survivor Records: www.survivor.co.uk
- Drummerworld: www.drummerworld.com

About the Author

Terl Bryant is an inspirational teacher, producer, drummer and percussionist. He is married to Juliet and they have five children and live in West Sussex, England. Terl has for many years played professionally in both the Christian and the mainstream music industries and is the founder of Psalm Drummers, a vision to inspire and release believing drummers in their gifts. His credits include touring and recording with John Paul Jones of Led Zeppelin, Iona, Matt Redman, Faith Hill, the Honeyz, Leslie Garrett, Maddy Prior and many more. He has recorded and produced several albums, including the CD & DVD 'Psalm Drummers' on Survivor Records UK (2004) and 'Drops of Glittering Hope' by Jules Bryant. Terl has a pastor's heart and is an insightful teacher in matters of faith.

Terl is endorsed by: Jalapeno drums (www.jalapenodrums.co.uk), Zildjian cymbals (zildjian.com), Remo percussion (remo.com), Promark sticks (promark.com), Hardcase (hardcase.com), Big Dog Stands (intimeperc.com), Malachy Bodhrans (bodhran.com), ACS monitoring, hearing protection (hearingprotection.co.uk) and DM Music (dmmusic.com)

Psalm Drummers: CD/DVD (SURCD098)

The release includes 8 exciting drumming pieces which reflect the character of drummers enjoying worship together. It is declarational, celebrational, spiritual and fun. Also including a bonus DVD which features over 60 drummers filmed at The Call in Reading and Terl teaching about the role of the drum in worship

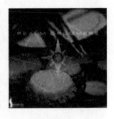

Facedown DVD: Matt Redman (SURDVD5007)

Join with a generation of worshippers who shout loud and bow low for the glory of God. 12 songs of passionate, reverent worship, 3 talks from Louie Giglio, global worship conversations with Matt Redman, Darleen Zschech, Graham Kendrick, & Louie Giglio, and 'Notes on songwriting' with Matt & Beth Redman, Tim Hughes and Mike Pilavachi.

Passion for Your Name: Tim Hughes (1842911759)

If you want to be more involved in leading worship in your church, or become a more effective member of the band, then this book is a great place to begin.

Worship, Evangelism/Justice:
Mike Pilavachi & Liza Hoeksma (1842912844)

This book looks at what happens when we let worship infuse all areas of our lives, what evangelism looks like in today's culture, and what God's passion for justice means in a broken and hurting world. God holds all three close to his heart: if we bring them back together, could we regain the lost voice of the church?

Inside-out Worship (1842912267) &
the Heart of Worship Files (1842911368):
Matt Redman & Friends

Containing invaluable guidance from some of today's most seasoned leaders and lead worshippers: Matt Redman, Louie Giglio, Robin Mark, Darlene Zschech, Brian Houston, Terl Bryant, Chris Tomlin, Paul Baloche and many more.